DORSET SHIPWRECKS

To my wife Carol

For in every sense this is her book, too

A GUIDE TO

DORSET SHIPWRECKS

FROM THE SOUTH WEST COAST PATH

TERRY TOWNSEND

ACKNOWLEDGEMENTS

Thanks to Brenda and Tony Stables
for their continued help and encouragement

Thanks also to Karen Binaccioni for her invaluable design input

First published in Great Britain in 2020

Copyright © Terry Townsend 2020

British Library Cataloguing-in-Publication Data
A CIP record for this title is available from the
British Library

ISBN 978 0 85710 123 5

PiXZ Books
Halsgrove House, Ryelands Business Park,
Bagley Road, Wellington, Somerset TA21 9PZ
Tel: 01823 653777
Fax: 01823 216796
email: sales@halsgrove.com

An imprint of Halstar Ltd, part of the
Halsgrove group of companies
Information on all Halsgrove titles is
available at: www.halsgrove.com

Printed and bound in India by
Parksons Graphics Pvt Ltd

CONTENTS

LOCATION MAP

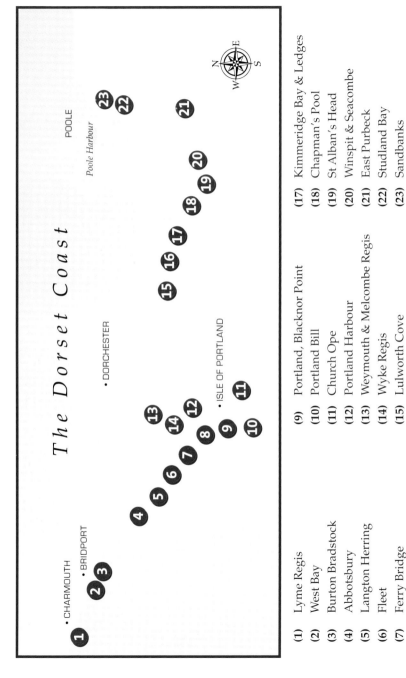

The Dorset Coast

(1) Lyme Regis
(2) West Bay
(3) Burton Bradstock
(4) Abbotsbury
(5) Langton Herring
(6) Fleet
(7) Ferry Bridge
(8) Chesil Cove, Chiswell

(9) Portland, Blacknor Point
(10) Portland Bill
(11) Church Ope
(12) Portland Harbour
(13) Weymouth & Melcombe Regis
(14) Wyke Regis
(15) Lulworth Cove
(16) Worbarrow Bay

(17) Kimmeridge Bay & Ledges
(18) Chapman's Pool
(19) St Alban's Head
(20) Winspit & Seacombe
(21) East Purbeck
(22) Studland Bay
(23) Sandbanks

INTRODUCTION

The Dorset Coast Path from Lyme Regis to Poole takes in some of the county's most popular beaches, romantic coves, sweeping bays and arresting cliff top scenery. However, long before leisure was a concept for working people, the path was established as a patrol route for Customs Riding Officers engaged in the suppression of smuggling.

Best known today for its Jurassic World Heritage status Dorset's infinitely varied coastline has a darker side being witness to prolonged tragedy. For as long as men have sailed the seas elements have conspired to destroy their ships. In addition to contending with gale force winds, mountainous waves and impenetrable fog, mariners of the Dorset coast faced additional hazards of sinister submerged sandbanks and razor sharp rocks.

This arresting view of Tilly Whim Caves can be seen from The Dorset Coast Path as it traverses the cliff tops between Anvil Point and Durlston Head.

Over many centuries craft of all types from around the world have run the gauntlet of the English Channel and fought a losing battle. East Indiamen, fishing smacks, treasure ships, paddle-steamers and emigrant vessels; all have ended their days off the Dorset coast. The hazardous Purbeck cliffs have claimed their share but the treacherous waters off Chesil Bank and the Isle of Portland have wrought the greatest destruction where giant seas have split vessels in two by sheer force of waves.

For centuries, Lyme Bay was considered the only safe anchorage for shelter during storms. Even so the seabed here is greatly littered with sunken ships and often referred to as '*The Bay of a Thousand Wrecks*'. During the days of sail, Chesil Beach frequently proved a death trap for any vessel caught in a winter storm. The chilling name '*Deadman's Bay*' is given to the point where the unforgiving shingle bank meets the iron fist of Portland. The 'Great Gales' of 1824 and 1838 took their toll as did conflicts during both world wars when man rendered the cruel sea even crueller.

Best known today for its Jurassic World Heritage status Dorset's infinitely varied coastline has a darker side being witness to prolonged tragedy.

Over many centuries craft of all types from around the world have run the gauntlet of the English Channel and fought a losing battle.

Selwyn Williams, experienced diver and author of *Treasure of the Golden Grape*, at an exhibition in Melcombe Regis Old Town Hall of marine artefacts discovered off the Dorset coast.

The sadly over-crowded churchyards along Dorset's seaboard confirm there is nothing remotely romantic about a shipwreck. However, there is often compelling drama bringing forth the best and worst of human responses. Here are stories behind some of the most gripping and unusual of Dorset's maritime disasters, revealing human error, individual heroism and wholesale looting by those drawn to the cry of *ship ashore!*

Although countless vessels have sunk without trace, over 400 Dorset shipwrecks are now known and wreck diving is a passion for many. The recovery of a stone anchor off Lulworth and discovery of Roman coins off Chesil suggest Roman galleys may be among the first of Dorset's shipwrecks and early as 877 over a hundred Viking longships were wrecked in Swanage Bay. The latest spectacular wreck discovery is a Spanish ship from the time of Columbus found in Studland Bay.

Finds from a period of over 2000 years continue to be recovered and displayed in local museums at Lyme Regis,

Bridport, Portland's Ope Cove, Weymouth, Swanage and Poole. Today support for those who find themselves in peril off Dorset's coast is provided by dedicated volunteers who crew those big orange lifesaving vessels strategically stationed at Lyme, Weymouth, Swanage and, of course Poole, home of the Royal National Lifeboat Institution.

Swanage volunteer lifeboat crew are ready 24/7 for the moment the distress siren sounds.

The harbour at Lyme Regis is formed by the encircling wall of The Cobb.

LYME REGIS

The shorelines of Devon and Dorset converge at a point on the Jurassic World Heritage Coast just west of Lyme Regis. The cliffs and beaches here reveal the Earth's history across 185 million years. Lyme's most striking feature however is only around 800 years old. The great stone-built curving breakwater known as The Cobb helps form the harbour but even this cannot protect sheltering vessels from the most ferocious storms.

Unity: 23 November 1824

Fierce winter gales have always been a fact of life for dwellers in Dorset's coastal communities, although nothing prepared them for the terrifying night of 22/23 November 1824 when a storm rose in the early hours to develop into a destructive hurricane recorded in history as the 'Great Gale'. This extraordinary meterological event left untold devastation in its path along the entire English Channel seaboard.

Lyme Bay in benign mood looking along The Cobb towards Charmouth and Golden Cap.

Howling winds ripped off roofs and chimneys and tore down whole buildings. Trees by the thousand were uprooted and cows and sheep drowned as rivers overflowed. At Lyme The Cobb was severely breached and several vessels were lost, including the London trader *Unity*. This was partly blamed on the government not investing sufficiently in repairs to the harbour wall in the wake of storms seven years earlier.

The London trader *Unity* being driven ashore at Lyme Regis during the Great Gale of 1824.

The extreme breaching of The Cobb left vessels sheltering within vulnerable to gale force winds and surging waves. An early casualty was a small fishing smack which, after losing its moorings, sank close to Crab Head. Shortly afterwards the 16 ton half-decked Lyme-built fishing smack *Caroline* was thrust out of the harbour grounding at the mouth of the River Lym where crashing breakers swiftly reduced it to match-wood. The next ship driven out of the anchorage was the single-decked 24 ton sloop *Mary Elizabeth* which was carried past the town to be stranded close to Church Cliff.

Watching the destruction from the cliff top was Captain Charles Bennett RN, a resident of Lyme. Around him stood a crowd of men, women and children, some still dressed in nightgowns, having just managed to escape from their houses before they collapsed. Every so often there was a cry as another house succumbed to pounding waves. The largest of

The Cobb warehouses was destroyed and the others severely damaged.

Captain Bennett watched helplessly as the revenue cutter *Fox* broke free from its moorings and collided with the harbour's north wall. The damaged vessel drifted helplessly and two of the four man crew could be seen clinging to the mast while the other two were drowned attempting to swim for their lives. Both were family men who between them left two grieving widows and eleven children. For a moment the ship seemed to run ahead of the wind before the waves completely engulfed it.

Bennett now focused his telescope on the trading vessel, *Unity* which was well known in Lyme. Every six weeks she sailed for London bringing back heavy goods to the otherwise poorly accessible town. Captain Pierce of the *Unity* was popular in Lyme and all his crew were local men. As Bennett watched in dismay, the stricken vessel was swept along by the ferocity of the storm firstly grounding below Church Cliff and finally being driven ashore midway between Lyme and Charmouth with the crew still on board.

Captain Bennett immediately began organising a small rescue party which included John Freeman and local pilot

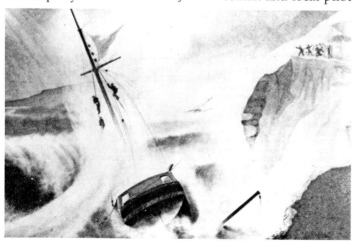

Cut from the rigging of the *Unity* an exhausted second seaman and the cabin boy both survived.
Drawing by Cater Galpin.

William Porter. Hastily collecting ropes they made their way as fast as possible along the cliff tops to affect a daring rescue. Porter was lowered down the cliff and managed to rescue Robert Pierce. Captain Bennett joined Porter at the cliffbase in time to pluck one of the crew from the sea at great risk to his own life. The two traumatised remaining crew members '*had to be cut from the rigging and bodily carried ashore*'.

In recognition of their bravery, the National Institution for the Preservation of Life for Shipwreck (later to become the RNLI) awarded Bennett a gold medal. Porter and Freeman were each presented with silver medals. The *Unity* was removed to Samuel Bussel's boatyard, the place of her launching in 1819. Remarkably, after undergoing repairs, she continued in the coasting trade and was last reported in 1854 working out of Fowey in Cornwall.

Heroine: Boxing Day 1852

On 29 September, 1852 the barque *Heroine* departed from London's East India Dock, bound for Port Philip (later Melbourne) Australia, with emigrants '*of the poorer class', plus 3000 fire-bricks as cargo in place of ballast*'. Within a few days she was in trouble after springing a leak off the Kent coast and limped westwards eventually reaching Portsmouth for repairs. During her stay in Portsmouth the structural problems with the ship were exacerbated when her master was replaced; suggesting the possibility of some discord aboard the vessel.

Once repaired, the *Heroine* continued westwards but met further problems on Christmas Eve in Torbay, crashing against a rock off 'Hope's Nose' during a fierce gale. Her rudder disabled, the barque drifted helplessly eastwards and a day and a half later the first reports of her distress were noticed off Beer Head. The *Heroine* carried two carronades (short iron cannons), and observers said they were used in addition to distress signals.

The stricken vessel was shipping water as it continued to be blown violently and uncontrollably across Lyme Bay. The new master, Captain Lerick, made the decision to abandon ship and all aboard took to the boats. In true seafaring tradition, Lerick was the last to leave. The people of Lyme were by now aware that they were witnessing a potential disaster. One reported that the ship 'sank three or four miles out, nearly opposite the town in 13 fathoms of water'.

The 1852 wreck of the Australian-bound emigrant ship *Heroine*, from a water-colour by William Bennett.

Meanwhile, three men from the revenue cutter *Frances* and two other mariners strapped cork to their waists as improvised lifejackets and launched the ship's pinnace (a light boat) to provide assistance. Sadly, the pinnace got no further than just outside the harbour mouth when it was overturned by the huge seas. Four of the five – Henry Cox, W. Harvey, H. Hearne and T. Black were drowned. One man, William Bridle, master of the *Primrose*, survived. Many of Lyme's residents witnessed the deaths of the men and one observer commented that the tragedy had 'cast a deep gloom over the town'.

Within a short time attention was drawn from despondency to jubilation when all the forty-three souls aboard the *Heroine* were saved as the ship's lifeboats made it to Church Beach. Ironically there were no casualties other than the Captain who had broken a leg while abandoning ship.

William Bridle, sole survivor of the pinnace was awarded a silver medal for his bravery and the RNLI donated £20 to a local fund for the dependants of the drowned men. The charity also agreed to pay a third of the cost of a lifeboat to be stationed in Lyme, and in 1853 ordered a 27-foot boat, which arrived in September of that year. There is a sad footnote however, as the hapless emigrants who survived the shipwreck were now destitute.

The 15,000 ton battleship HMS *Formidable*, was torpedoed in Lyme Bay on New Year's Day 1915 with the loss of 551 lives.

HMS *Formidable:* New Year's Day 1915

On New Year's Day in 1915 the Royal Navy battleship *Formidable* was torpedoed by a German submarine off Start Point in South Devon with the loss of more than 500 men. In a storm that followed the tragic incident, a life raft containing bodies was blown along the coast to Lyme Regis. Local pub The Pilot Boat made its cellar available as a makeshift mortuary.

The landlord's dog, a crossbred collie called Lassie, found her way down amongst the seven sailors who were laid out on the cellar floor. All were presumed dead but Lassie began to lick the face of one of the victims, Able Seaman John Cowan. The dog stayed beside the motionless mariner for more than half an hour, nuzzling him and keeping him warm with her body until, to everyone's astonishment, Cowan eventually stirred and was taken to hospital where he made a full recovery. He visited Lassie again when he returned to Lyme to thank all who saved his life.

The sinking of the ship was a severe blow to Britain during the early years of the First World War. When the officers heard the inspirational and heart-warming story of Lassie and what she did to resuscitate Cowan, they told it again and again to any reporter who would listen. It seems likely it provided inspiration for Yorkshire novelist and screenwriter Eric Knight who is mainly known for his Lassie adventure books; particularly his 1938 novel *Lassie Come-Home*, which introduced the fictional brave hearted collie.

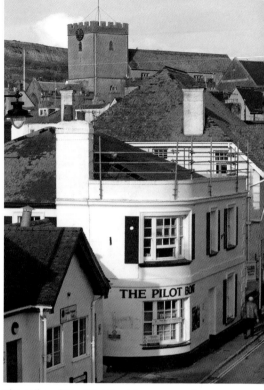

The cellar of The Pilot Boat Inn was used as a makeshift mortuary for victims of the torpedoed HMS *Formidable*.

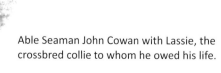

Able Seaman John Cowan with Lassie, the crossbred collie to whom he owed his life.

Lyme's saddest day as the townsfolk turned out to pay their respects to the victims of the HMS *Formidable* disaster.

The *Heroine* disaster helped to accelerate the provision of a lifeboat for Lyme eventually leading to the installation of this third generation Atlantic 85 B-class Rigid Inflatable.

2

WEST BAY

The market town of Bridport lies a mile-and-a-half inland from its harbour. Historically the town needed a harbour to export its principal products of rope and nets and to import the goods and materials required for its growth and prosperity. The harbour is not a natural landscape feature and has a long history of silting up, being blocked by shingle and damaged by storms. Following each event, repairs, improvements and enlargements were made.

The location of the harbour itself has changed three times. It was originally one mile inland and later relocated to the coast beside East Cliff. In 1740 a four-year building project commenced to construct a new harbour 300 yards to the west which when completed could accommodate forty sailing ships. By 1830 over 500 vessels were using the harbour each year.

West Bay on a benign summer day with its dramatic golden-coloured East Cliff as background.

When a fierce south-westerly wind is blowing West Bay presents a formidable challenge to sailors.

No Dorset port however was as hazardous to enter or exit and crews who worked the stone ships in particular risked death on every voyage. With the coming of the Great Western Railway in 1884 Bridport Harbour was promoted as a holiday resort and the name changed to West Bay to help attract visitors.

Black Diamond: November 1865

The Bull Hotel in the town centre is connected to a fictional West Bay drowning and two real life shipwrecks. Thomas Hardy's short story *Fellow Townsmen* is set in Bridport which he calls *Port Bredy*. George Barnet, the principal character, stays at Hardy's *Black-Bull Hotel*. The harbour and the road linking it to the town feature significantly in the story. The plot hinges on a drowning at West Bay but the victim revives hours later. We have already seen with the case of Able Seaman John Cowan at Lyme Regis this can happen in real life.

By the time in November 1865, when the Cork schooner *Black Diamond* was wrecked on West Bay beach, The Bull had established itself as one of the most famous coaching inns in the West Country. It had extensive stabling and a consequential requirement for large quantities of fodder. The schooner's cargo of Irish oats destined for the inn was lost with the wreck but thankfully the crew were saved. Five years later, a second schooner, the *Kennet*, was lost on the same part of the beach carrying an identical cargo which again was bound for The Bull Hotel.

Alioth: April 1923

It is ironic when the story of a wreck can raise a smile but such was the case in May 1923 when the German Ketch *Alioth* was

The German Ketch *Alioth* aground in May 1923 after the captain declined an offer by a local steam tug to tow her out of the harbour and clear of land.

23

preparing to leave sheltered anchorage of *West Bay*. The captain, looking for a speedy turn around, wished to sail immediately despite the fact a strong south west wind was blowing across the harbour entrance. The iron-clad sailing vessel was one of many small ships that delivered and collected cargo from West Bay. On this occasion she had unloaded timber and was taking on board a load of local sand and, as always with commercial transport, time was money.

A local pilot boat offered a tow out of the harbour for the price of 10/- (50p) which was common practice. The captain declined and instructed his crew to push the ship out of port using oars and poles. No sooner had she cleared the harbour entrance than the vessel ran aground. The incoming tide

Two piers extending as far as the low tide mark present the difficult entrance to West Bay harbour.

Only fishing boats and pleasure craft moor in West Bay harbour today.

failed to float her off and she became stranded on East Beach. The wind increased with the waves crashing into the ship and in a short time she was wrecked as the dramatic photograph shows.

The captain had been advised to take advantage of the reasonably priced tow by the steam tug and only to set sail when he was well offshore. No one was killed, but one wonders how the captain explained the loss to the ship's owners.

During the stagecoach era the Bull Inn in Bridport town centre had extensive stabling and required substantial quantities of Irish oats to feed the horses.

The western extent of Chesil Beach known as Burton Hive.

3

BURTON BRADSTOCK

Approaching from West Bay, Burton signifies the beginning of the 18-mile long pebble and shingle 'tombolo' of Chesil, bounding the cruellest lee shore in Dorset. The Saxons gave us the word 'Chesil' meaning shingle. The term tombolo is derived from the Latin tumulus, meaning 'mound', a deposition landform in which an island is attached to the mainland by a narrow piece of land such as a spit or bar. No other stretch of coast in the British Isles has resulted in so many deaths by shipwreck; over two hundred vessels are known to have come to grief here and the actual total is certainly much higher.

The beach is at its most lethal in a southwesterly gale, and once embayed and certain of striking, a prudent captain would order his helmsman to run hard ashore in the hope of grounding the ship's bow as high as possible on the bank in desperate hope his crew might scramble ashore and escape the lethal undertow. In January 1629 a Spanish ship ran aground here and was extensively looted. Remains of the wreck have been found off Hive Beach where several iron cannon were discovered.

Other known vessels to have come to grief here at Burton Hive include a Danish Brig, wrecked in November 1824. In 1829 it was the fate of the *Magnet* and in March 1832 the *Swallow* was lost. In November 1838 the French smack *Le Mercura* grounded and in August 1879 the Brig *Endeavour* suffered the same fate. On 23 November 1837 a Swedish Brig, the *Systrarne* was wrecked under Burton Cliffs. On this occasion several men were saved and the vicar noted with pleasure how his parishioners had exerted themselves in descending the cliffs with ropes to save the unfortunate sailors, rather than just loot the wreck.

Flirt: 1898

Early in the night of Wednesday 23 November 1898, a northeast breeze had been blowing but veered round to develop into a very strong southerly gale. A mountainous sea was soon running, and the wind increased in violence during the day. The 150 ton schooner *Flirt*, of Whitstable, had been bound from London to Topsham with 240 tons of copper ore. On the night of Tuesday 22nd she was down off Exmouth hoping for a tug to tow her into harbour but at midnight she was caught by the southerly gale and lost all her sails. She then drifted helplessly about, at the mercy of the wind and sea, till she came ashore at Hive Beach at 4 p.m. on Wednesday afternoon.

An hour earlier William Smith was on Burton church tower looking for the approach of a funeral cortege from West Bay. He spotted the *Flirt* and was startled to see her close inshore with all her sails blown away. An alarm was raised, and men and women were quickly on the cliff and beach ready to render assistance. An account published in *The Burton and Shipton Gorge Parish Magazine* of December 1898 described the scene:

A shed opposite the former Dove Inn served as a mortuary for victims of frequent drownings at Burton Hive beach.

'The wind was at its height, and the seas tremendous, as they rolled in and broke with deafening roars on the shingle. At a glance the most experienced could see there was no chance for the little vessel, which was being tossed about like a cork some 300 yards from the beach, and there also appeared but little probability that the poor men clinging to the main rigging could ever reach the land in safety. After a short time it was seen that the vessel was being headed straight for the shore, and it appeared at first as if she would be beached in the middle of the Hive. When, however, the vessel was some 200 yards from the shore, a huge wave struck her aft and completely hid her from view; when she reappeared her decks had been swept, her wheel carried away, and she had broached broadside on the sea, and was heading for the cliffs to the westward. The next distressing sight was to see four men jump from the rigging into the boiling seas. For many minutes the sailors in their life jackets made good way to the shore, being pushed in by the ever-breaking billows'.

The table with its one piece solid elm top is now housed in the village reading room behind the present day Three Horseshoes pub.

With and without lifelines, villagers made the most courageous rescue attempts and three of the crew of six were saved. A hatch cover from the wreck was used as a makeshift stretcher to carry the bodies to the village pub. The pub at that time was The Dove which today is two private dwellings – The Cider House and Smugglers' Cottage.

Corpses carried up to the village on the elm hatch cover were Captain Chedwick, who left a widow and a little daughter, the mate, Rigden, a single man, and the apprentice Hare, an orphan on his first voyage. They were laid out in a shed opposite the pub which served for years as a mortuary for victims of the frequent drownings. The hatch cover was later fashioned into a table top for the Dove where it was intended to remain but sadly the popular pub closed in recent years.

4

ABBOTSBURY

The Rev'd William Alleyne Barker was vicar of Abbotsbury from 1822 until his death in 1831. Two years into the job, in the aftermath of the 1824 storm, Barker found and buried 18 sailors washed up on the beach. He was so shocked by the event he decided to devote all his energies to preventing such dreadful things happening again. With the help of the National Institution for the Preservation of Life from Shipwreck (in 1854 renamed the Royal National Lifeboat Institution) he was instrumental in establishing the first lifeboats in Dorset.

Rev'd William Alleyne Barker devoted all his energies to establishing the first lifeboats in Dorset.

The village of Abbotsbury is situated about 1 mile inland from the coast near the halfway point on Chesil Beach.

Approaching from the west the first of sight of Abbotsbury is the famous landmark of St Catherine's Chapel with a view of Fleet Water, Chesil Beach and the English Channel.

Mary Ann: 1838

During severe gales that hit the Dorset coast on 28 November 1838 more than a dozen vessels were wrecked with loss of life. At Abbotsbury a Plymouth schooner, the *Mary Ann* was wrecked. Four men and a boy were drowned, one man, John Randall, was saved.

Dorothea: 1914

A number of vessels washed up on Dorset beaches over the years were not technically 'wrecks' as such, because they were temporarily stranded and subsequently refloated. When the SS *Dorothea*, of Rotterdam, went ashore near Abbotsbury during the night of 14/15 February 1914, the crew were able to walk ashore at low water. Two dogs, a Pomeranian and a Dachshund, were also rescued, carried in a pillowcase from the beached vessel.

The ship was carrying a cargo of iron ore from Spain to Holland and, despite the combined weight of vessel and cargo storm force waves carried it broadside on high up the beach where she remained stranded for two years. The *Dorothea* was eventually salvaged when baulks of timber were placed under her keel to form 'slip ways' and two tugs, one on the bow and one on the stern hauled her towards the sea. As she progressed down the beach the operation was repeated.

During the operation a gale force wind began to blow, whipping up a nasty sea pounding the *Dorothea* and buckling her plates and frames. Had the heavy weather continued they would probably have lost her but fortunately the weather abated and when dragging resumed she was successfully launched broadside from the beach but with rather a nasty list. Once properly afloat she was ballasted, put on an even keel and subsequently towed to a dock for repair. The *Dorothea* was eventually sold to a shipping company and employed in the London Newcastle coal trade. While on a voyage in the North Sea in 1916 she struck a mine and sank but luckily the crew were saved.

This photograph of Dutch steamer *Dorothea* aground on Chesil Beach near Abbotsbury in February 1914 conveys some idea of the power of the storm force waves.

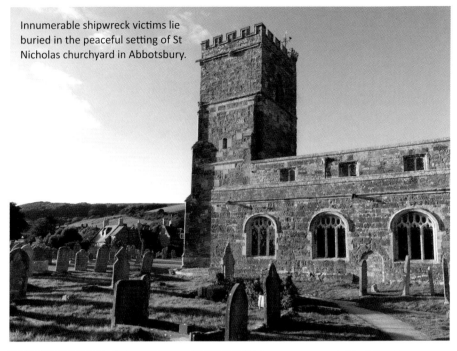

Innumerable shipwreck victims lie buried in the peaceful setting of St Nicholas churchyard in Abbotsbury.

Abbotsbury today is best known for its swannery, subtropical gardens and surviving abbey buildings. In the past this extensive section of open beach has claimed a dreadful toll on shipping.

LANGTON HERRING

The small fishing village of Langton Herring lies 5½ miles northwest of Weymouth. The name comes from the Old English 'Lang + tun' meaning 'long farmstead or estate' with the thirteenth century Lords of the Manor family name 'Harang' attached. There is no direct access to Chesil Beach from the village without first crossing Fleet Water.

Coastguard cottages at Langton Herring near the site of the mass graves where 300 victims of Admiral Christian's Fleet lie buried.

Six ships of Admiral Christian's fleet:
Thursday 19 November 1795

As dawn broke on Thursday 19 November 1795 William Shrapnel, a surgeon with the South Gloucester Militia crossed Fleet Water to access Chesil Beach and came upon an unimaginably horrific scene. The aftermath of the destruction of six ships hurled against the steeply-banked shingle during a ferocious storm the previous night. The vessels involved were:

Chesil Beach with Fleet Water on one side and the Channel on the other was strewn for 2 miles with the wreckage of ships and corpses of men, women, horses and other animals.

The Catherine of Montrose, The Aeolus of Whitby, The Golden Grove of London, The Piedmont, The Venus, and The Thomas of London.

Shrapnel described the scene that greeted him as he reached the top of the bank:

'the wind was still roaring and the sea still turbulent; for a mile in each direction along the beach was the strewn wreckage of ships. In addition to the corpses of men and women, there were horses and other animals. In the violently tossing sea floated more corpses, the waves occasionally tossing them up on the beach to join the others. The bodies were stripped naked of their clothes, either by the sea or scavengers, the skin ripped and bruised, mutilated beyond recognition, some no longer had faces. And amongst these corpses, local people moved about, still scavenging implacably for goods'.

The vessels were part of the greatest fleet of ships to leave Britain's shores. In 1795 the French were threatening British supremacy in the West Indies and in November that year the task force commanded by Admiral Sir Hugh Clobbery Christian embarked from Spithead with the intention of re-establishing authority.

The fleet's departure had been delayed until late in the season and did not set sail until 16 November. The delay proved disastrous: two days after departing the massive flotilla sailed into the worst storm for a century. Some of the ships were

blown backwards from one end of the English Channel to the other in the teeth of the westerly gale. For weeks afterwards the sea cast up dead bodies and untold pieces of wreckage.

Admiral Christian's fleet of 200 vessels sailed from Spithead in 1795 to re-establish supremacy in the West Indies but ran into the worst storm for a century.

Men of the Gloucester Militia encamped on the downs above Weymouth were delegated the task of digging mass graves on the landward side of Chesil for the 300 odd ordinary soldiers and sailors. Women and those of the men who could be identified as officers were buried in Wyke Regis churchyard (see chapter 14). The expeditionary force finally sailed again between mid-February and mid-March. During May and June the British succeeded in capturing St Lucia, Saint Vincent, and Grenada.

The Golden Grove

This was a slave ship bound for St Kitts. Two years earlier under Captain John Proudfoot the vessel made a successful voyage to the Bight of Benin gathering slaves and delivering them to Jamaica. When wrecked at Chesil much of the vessel's valuable cargo of 'trade goods' was lost. These goods were intended to be used as currency to barter for African natives.

The Catherine

On the troop transport *Catherine*, one of only two survivors was a young woman left destitute by the tragedy which

Mrs Burns, visible on the quarter deck of the *Catherine*, was one of only two survivors of the forty souls on board.

drowned forty other souls on board, including her husband Cornet* William Stukely Burns of the 26th Light Dragoons. Stukely was an American whose allegiance to the British flag had led to his disinheritance and consequently his wife was left destitute. However, her first-hand account of the awful experience was used by Charlotte Smith, a popular literary figure of the time, in her *Narrative of the Wrecks of Admiral Christian's Fleet* with the subscription price going to Mrs Burns.

Admiral Sir Hugh Clobbery Christian, commander of the ill-fated fleet.

Mrs Charlotte Smith who used Mrs Burns' eye witness account of the disaster to write a narrative of the tragic event.

Cornet was originally the third and lowest grade of commissioned officer in a British cavalry troop, after Captain and Lieutenant.

6

FLEET

The severe gales of 23 November 1824 formed huge seas so powerful they breached Chesil Bank and flooded Fleet village. Many buildings were destroyed or damaged and the Old Church suffered greatly. Victorian author John Meade Falkner, who was brought up in Dorchester and Weymouth, used the Great Storm as background to his classic adventure novel *Moonfleet*. Built in 1603 by Maximillian Mohune, Fleet House (now Moonfleet Manor Hotel), stands on the edge of Fleet Water at the end of a minor road.

The Hope: 1749

On 16 January 1749 the Dutch East Indiaman, *Hope* was wrecked opposite Fleet. Laden with gold, silver and other treasures estimated to be worth more than £4 million she was the richest vessel ever to be destroyed in a storm on Chesil Beach.

The *Hope* had set sail from Amsterdam on the 17 April 1747 bound for the Dutch owned Caribbean island of Curaçao. She went on to sail on the Spanish Main; the stretch of coastline in the Americas controlled by Spain in the sixteenth through to the eighteenth-centuries. Here she sold her cargo to Spaniards who were eager to replenish supplies depleted in consequence of war with England.

With business concluded Captain Corneliz and his 73 man crew were headed for home and arrived off Portland on the 16 January 1748. They had sailed through storms and tempestuous seas during the previous fourteen days. Fearing his treasure ship, now loaded with gold, jewels and other valuable

Captain Corneliz'
crew carried
some salvaged
goods to Fleet
House (now
Moonfleet
Manor Hotel).

commodities, might be a target for pirates or the English Navy, Corneliz had all 30 of the ship's guns mounted ready for action.

It was around one or two o'clock in the morning and very dark when the *Hope* ran ashore on Chesil Beach opposite Fleet House. Perhaps it was due to channel mist, or possible neglect of duty – there was no light visible from Portland lighthouse. Whatever the reason, she struck land with such force of impact the mast fell and the ship shattered into three parts. The upper deck was thrown upon a ridge of pebbles and the cabin buried in the sands; the hull was never found and thought to have rolled back into the sea. Amazingly, all the men aboard scrambled safely to shore. Word of what had happened quickly spread and the whole countryside within a radius of 20 miles was organised to plunder. Looters from Dorset and neighbouring counties flocked to the area hopeful of securing any washed up goods.

The men of Portland, Wyke and Weymouth were first on the scene. With a well-rehearsed shipwreck drill they formed into groups of 20, each uniting under a leader to secure the goods floating along the coast. A report written later suggests there were hundreds of local men employed in this endeavour and others arrived from farther afield swelling the numbers to several thousand.

These few remaining cottages along Butter Street are vestiges of Fleet Village devastated in the Great Storm of 1824.

For ten days the mob held the beach. One report described: *'a scene of unheard of riot, violence and barbarity'*. Another account said: *'a crowd swarmed about the water's edge grubbing for gold, tearing up the shingle with their bare nails, fighting over gleaming coins like starved wolves'*. Troops sent to guard the cargo were overwhelmed and for more than a week there were wild scenes along the beach with several men dying of exposure after looting the ship's spirit store. On 20 January several bags of money were found six feet under the pebbles.

This small chancel chapel is all that survived when the body of the church was destroyed in the storm.

Eventually, after ten days, three neighbouring Justices of the Peace with a body of armed men managed to disperse the mob. An inquiry was held and the authorities set about tracing the possessors of the plundered goods. Looters were compelled to hand over gold, jewellery and other goods valued between £25,000 and £30,000 to the agent for Dutch merchant firm Hendrick Hogenberg and Co. The plunderers were allowed something for salvage rights.

Some men were committed to prison and two appeared before Judge Baron Heneage Legge at Dorchester assizes on 15 July 1749 but were acquitted. The jury accepted the men's claim that the Dutch were pirates and therefore plunder was legal. The jury also took into account that only two men stood before them when all manner of disorders were committed by many of the reported thousands present on the beach during those ten lawless days and nights.

When the *Hope* struck land the mast fell with such force of impact that the ship shattered into three parts. Amazingly, all of the men aboard scrambled safely to the shore.

The court was told Augustine Elliott of Portland, was the principal organiser of the army of looters: '*He was the muster-master, the treasurer, and divider of the prey amongst his plundering regiment*'. However, his defence council successfully argued that, in the whole affair, his client acted an open and public spirited part: '*What he assisted in carrying away home was with an intention to save and not destroy; to preserve for the owners and not to steal and keep from them. On this generous fixed principle he not only acted himself but to his utmost laboured to bring the company he was concerned with to behave in the same humane and honest manner*'. Elliott's trial lasted six hours and thirty minutes and the jury brought in a verdict of 'NOT GUILTY'.

It emerged from the court hearing that Captain Corneliz and part of his crew carried some salvaged goods to Fleet House, hoping they would be protected by the King's Officers but it seems they were disappointed.

On 25 November 1872 the iron sailing ship *Royal Adelaide* was wrecked on Chesil Beach opposite Ferry Bridge.

FERRY BRIDGE

Prior to 1839, when the gap between Portland and the mainland was bridged, Portland was a true island. The small strait in between was a notoriously treacherous crossing, where people and animals alike were ferried across in small boats and later by a rope-drawn ferry. This ferry was destroyed by the fearsome storm that hit the Dorset coast in late November 1824. The ferryman's cottage was ripped apart by the fury of the waves and swept away. Richard Best, the ferryman with over thirty years experience, drowned whilst struggling to rescue a stranded horse.

Rev'd Chamberlaine, rector of Wyke Regis, noted the sandbank which had previously enabled horses and wagons to drive across to the island at low water was completely washed away making the gap between Wyke and Portland four times as wide. For some days, Portland was completely cut off and the wild waters eroded Chesil's pebbled bank lowering it by some twenty to thirty feet.

Royal Adelaide: 25 November 1872

On 25 November 1872 the iron sailing ship *Royal Adelaide* was wrecked on Chesil Beach opposite Ferry Bridge, rolling broadside in the breakers towards the Beach. The 1400 ton ship built by William Patterson of Bristol in 1865 was on a passage from London to Sydney with a crew of 32 plus 35 emigrant passengers bound for a new life in Australia.

On the night of 24 November the *Royal Adelaide* was reported to have passed the Portland lighthouse – perhaps a little too close off its starboard bow for comfort. When the weather deteriorated to gale force the ship's captain, William Hunter, tried to reach the shelter of Portland Harbour but by the afternoon of the 25th she was forced into Lyme Bay from which there was no escape. The anchors were lowered in an effort to prevent the ship being blown onto the western end of Chesil Beach but they dragged and she began breaking up on the great shingle bank.

The first mate drowned whilst desperately trying to swim ashore with a line. Those watching from the beach could do nothing until the stricken vessel was close enough to fire a line on board. Rocket apparatus was set up and a group of

The rope-drawn ferry operating between the mainland and the Island of Portland was destroyed in 1824 by the fearsome storm that hit the Dorset coast in late November.

45

A painting showing the scene at the western end of Chesil Beach after the 200 ton emigrant clipper *Royal Adelaide* was driven broadside onto the beach during the south-westerly gale.

Portlanders linked by ropes successfully tossed a line aboard. Once the cradle was rigged up the rescue began despite the dreadful conditions sixty people were brought ashore. News soon spread of the helpless ship off Chesil and local people rushed to witness the dramatic scene lighting the beach with tar barrels and blue flares. Many others arrived on the packed 5 p.m. train from Weymouth. It was thought 3000 people (both men and women) gathered along the shore to witness the last rights of the *Royal Adelaide*.

Captain Hunter was first to use the cradle. He made this decision after realising most passengers were too terrified to trust their lives to the seemingly fragile basket, but seeing him land safely they followed his example. The last passengers to leave the ship were a married couple with a young child who had steadfastly refused to use the basket. However, a man holding a child in his arms was seen entering the cradle but tragically the line broke and they were pitched into the sea; the two bodies were never recovered. The final person to be rescued was the second mate.

As the vessel began breaking up its cargo started to float ashore. First came hats, soap, candles, coffee, then some livestock – it was reported one pig survived by swimming to safety. Almost immediately scuffles broke out as people on the beach began to scramble for the goods in a mad frenzy. When finally casks and bottles of spirits were washed up the scene became one of drunken debauchery.

The wholesale plunder and unbridled drinking by the aggressive looters could not be prevented by the vastly outnumbered coastguards, police and military. The following morning the roll call of at least one local school was abandoned as most of the children had joined their parents treasure hunting on Chesil Beach. Some stolen goods were later buried in gardens.

The rescue harness being used to bring ashore passengers and crew from the ill-fated *Royal Adelaide.*

All but six of the emigrant passengers and crew were saved but it was estimated that double that number of spectators died from drunkenness or exposure as they slept off their excess on the beach through a bitterly cold night.

A group photograph of the grim-faced men who survived the wreck of the *Royal Adelaide.*

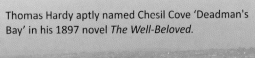
Thomas Hardy aptly named Chesil Cove 'Deadman's Bay' in his 1897 novel *The Well-Beloved*.

8

CHESIL COVE, CHISWELL

Chesil Beach curves sharply at the eastern end, near the village of Chiswell, forming Chesil Cove backed by the cliffs of the Isle of Portland. Traditionally a fishing village, Chiswell is the island's oldest settlement and has been vulnerable to flooding for centuries. Modern coastal defence work began with the construction of a sea wall in 1958-65 with additional measures added during the 1980s.

This notorious maritime hazard has been the scene of so many shipwrecks the stories would fill volumes. It can be tempestuous, it can be serene but even in its stillness there's

Just beyond The Cove House Inn, Chesil Beach curves sharply forming the unforgiving maritime trap of Chesil Cove backed by the cliffs of the Isle of Portland.

something disconcerting here. Novelist John Fowles described it as: *'an elemental place, made of sea, shingle and sky, its dominant sound always that of waves on moving stone: from the great surf and pounding'.* In his 1897 novel *The Well-Beloved*, Thomas Hardy aptly named Chesil Cove *Deadman's Bay,* and described the scene witnessed by his two main characters Jocelyn Pierston and Avice Caro:

The Madelaine Tristan bar in Cove House Inn with its picture gallery of ships driven ashore on the beach.

> *'To the left of them the sky was streaked like a fan with the lighthouse rays, and under their front, at periods of a quarter of a minute, there arose a deep, hollow stroke like the single beat of a drum, the intervals being filled with a long-drawn rattling, as of bones between huge canine jaws. It came from the vast concave of Deadman's Bay, rising and falling against the pebble dyke'.*

A great fleet of fated vessels of every kind including two masted schooners, three masted barques and iron steam ships

This 2014 photograph captures the ferocity of a storm at Chesil Cove and demonstrates how the undertow creates the extraordinarily high waves.

have all succumbed to the turbulent seas off Deadman's Bay. Some idea of the scale of maritime destruction can be seen in photographs displayed on the wall of the *Madelaine Tristan* bar in Cove House Inn. The starkly named 'Dead House', still stands adjacent to a corner of the Cove House Inn car park. Corpses washed up on the beach were routinely laid out here or in the cellar of the inn before being taken off for burial.

Emma Maria: 25 October 1903

The Latvian schooner, *Emma Maria* was lost on 25 October 1903 with her cargo of china-clay. Tugs went to the aid of the vessel which had left Teignmouth for Lisbon but in the worsening weather it proved impossible to tow her to safety and she was left anchored at Blacknor on Portland's west coast. In the increasing gales the Russian ship dragged her anchors and was driven on to Chesil. As her mainmast snapped it fell across the beach, allowing the crew to scramble to safety.

Patria: 26 October 1903

The following day the Norwegian barque *Patria* was in trouble. She was on a voyage from Frederikstad to Port Natal with a cargo of timber when she lost her sails and was unable to round Portland Bill. Her captain decided his best chance

The wreck of *Patria* 1903. A rocket line enabled the crew to be rescued but the second mate had a leg amputated and the cook had to be restrained when he went mad.

was to run the ship onto the shingle and gave the order: 'Sea boots off and every man for himself'. The use of a rocket line enabled the crew to be rescued but the second mate had a leg amputated and the cook went mad and had to be restrained.

In his autobiography *Sea Fever*, A .H. Ramussen recalled his rescue:

Chesil Cove littered with cargo from the *Patria*.

'One moment I was riding the wave of a great comber and then it would suddenly break under me and hurl me head-long into a welter of boiling surf and shingle, suck me back, lift me up and toss me down again. How long I was tossed about I don't know. I only remember dimly that I saw a man running towards me through that deadly surf with a rope round his waist. The next moment a great cheer came from the beach as he grabbed me, and dozens of willing hands hauled us in'.

The two sections of the Greek owned *Preveza* after it broke up during a storm in 1920. The boilers remained visible for many years.

Preveza: 15 January 1920

The Greek-owned steamer *Preveza* collected coal and stores at Portland but failed to pay for them when she left for Cardiff. At the Welsh port she was refused entry as she was uninsured. Returning to Rotterdam the vessel became enveloped in dense fog in Chesil Cove and went aground broadside on to the beach. Local creditors vainly nailed writs to the mast and tried to salvage her but heavy seas did their worst and she eventually broke up. The boilers remained on the beach and were a local landmark for many years and traces of them still lie underneath the shingle.

Madelaine Tristan: September 1930

The last of the big sailing ships lost on the Dorset Coast was the French schooner *Madelaine Tristan*, wrecked at Chesil in September 1930. She was carrying a cargo of grain from Lorient in Brittany to Le Havre when several gales blew her hopelessly off course. In tremendous seas her skilful captain ran her up the beach on what he first assumed to be the north coast of France.

The master and his crew of six were soon rescued but the ship slewed round in the continuing gales eventually becoming a total wreck, remaining beached in the cove for five years. One local fisherman wistfully recalled: '*She was the finest prettiest sailing ship ever to come ashore on these coasts*'. In the accompanying picture the three masts and some of the rigging are still visible so it was probably taken during the first two years after the incident.

The *Madelaine Tristan* wrecked in September 1930 remained beached in the Cove for five years.

The *Emma Maria* was wrecked in the October gales of 1903.

The starkly named 'Dead House', adjacent to a corner of the Cove House Inn car park served for years as a mortuary.

Looking north across the erosional indentation of Mutton Cove towards Blacknor Point.

9

PORTLAND, BLACKNOR POINT

From Chiswell the Coast Path follows a southerly route along the top of the cliffs down the western side of Portland. Midway along the island's western shore centuries of coastal erosion have carved out Mutton Cove leaving Westcliff projecting forward creating the wicked promontory of Blacknor Point. Mutton Cove has been a graveyard for many ships driven onto the rocks ahead of a southwesterly storm. The precipitous cliffs made rescue extraordinarily difficult.

Ehen: 1890

In 1890 the French barque *Ehen* eventually became a total wreck after being stranded on rocks in Mutton Cove. The vessel was sailing from Bremerhaven heading for Bordeaux with a cargo of rice and preserves.

The French Barque *Ehen* aground in 1890 eventually became a total wreck.

Gertrude: 26 August 1894

In August 1894 the steamship *Gertrude* on a voyage from Huelva (Spain) to Rotterdam was carrying a cargo of iron pyrites when she drove ashore in dense fog between Tar Rocks and Blacknor Point. Fortunately the weather being calm there was no loss of life; the crew and two passengers were saved. The ship's cargo was jettisoned but she was unable to be refloated.

At the enquiry into the wreck it was determined insufficient use had been made of the 'lead and line' to determine the depth and no proper use made of the compass. The wreck site today is marked by the steamer's boiler which can be seen at low tide together with a mass of broken steel plate and an anchor, all scattered amongst the remains of her cargo.

55

The steamship *Gertrude* sinking after being stranded in thick fog on Blacknor Point in August 1894.

Patroclus: 13 September 1907

The 5500 ton steamer *Patroclus* belonging to the Ocean Steamship Company was bound from Brisbane with general cargo when it went ashore in fog near Blacknor Point on the morning of the 13 September 1907. No lives were lost but tugs sent to her assistance were initially unable to move her. Just over a week later the combined efforts of four tugs, a salvage vessel and 11 steam pumps finally managed to refloat the stranded steamer.

The 5500 ton *Patroclus*, bound from Brisbane with a general cargo including wool and bananas after striking Blacknor Point on 13 September 1907.

Myrtledene: March 1912

The British cargo vessel *Myrtledene*, ran aground in dense fog in March. Her crew were rescued by tug and attempts to refloat the vessel were soon made. However, due to the fact she was badly holed and *'so firmly embedded in the rocks'*, she was considered a total loss. Today, the remains of the ship lie broken up.

The German steamer *Okahandja* on Blacknor Point in June 1910. Much of her cargo had to be jettisoned before she could be refloated.

Bulow: June 1914

In June 1914, the German Norddeutscher Lloyd liner *Bulow* was on her way from Yokohama to Southampton with more than 300 passengers on board when she struck in the cove in foggy conditions. Her sirens brought most of Portland's inhabitants to the clifftop. When the fog lifted they gazed with some amazement at this magnificent vessel aground in Mutton Cove. Although the liner appeared to be in no imme-diate danger initial attempts to refloat her failed. All her

The German liner *Bulow* came to grief here in June 1914 with more than 300 passengers on board.

passengers were swiftly taken off and conveyed by steamer to Weymouth Pier to complete their journey to Southampton by train.

The *Bulow* was later successfully refloated and towed to Portland Harbour to reload cargo previously removed. Having suffered some minor damage to her hull, she then headed to Bremen for repairs.

The speedy evacuation of the passengers was no doubt influenced by news of the shocking maritime disaster which occurred two weeks earlier in Canada. Following a collision in the St Lawrence Seaway, the liner *Empress of Ireland* went down drowning more than a thousand souls on board. The dead included Weymouth jeweller John Vincent and his wife who were homeward bound after visiting relatives in Quebec.

James Fennel: 16 January 1920

The Admiralty steam trawler *James Fennell* was built in 1918 by the Paisley based firm of Fullerton & Co. She was lost in thick fog and drove straight on to rocks north of Blacknor point. All the crew were rescued by local fishermen using a long rope strung from the stem of the ship and anchored to a large rock. A few days later an attempt was made to tow the vessel off but she slid down the bank and sank immediately. The stern is complete and still attached to the bow, but is twisted. Huge boulders among the wreck make identification difficult but even so it is a favourite exploration site for scuba divers.

SS *James Fennell* ran aground and sunk in 1920. All the crew were rescued by local fishermen.

The *Forest* and *Avalanche* collided 12 miles southwest of Portland Bill during a violent storm on the night of 11 September 1877.

PORTLAND BILL

Portland Bill is a narrow promontory (or bill) at the southern end of the Isle of Portland, and the southernmost point of Dorset. The dangerous coastline here features shallow reefs and the Shambles sandbank. It is made even more hazardous for shipping due to the Portland Ledge, a submerged mass of Portland stone extending into the Channel, disrupting the tidal flow and causing the turbulent current known as the Portland Race which stops only for brief periods during the tidal cycle, reaching 4 metres per second at the spring tide. Three lighthouses have been built here to protect shipping. The original two worked as a pair from 1716, and were replaced in 1906 by the current one.

In addition to these natural hazards the Bill is a busy shipping lane and an important waypoint for coastal traffic. A number of ships have been involved in collisions here in bad weather and poor visibility. In June 1883 two New Zealand ships, the *Waitara* and *Hurunui* collided. The *Waitara* sank in about four minutes, and twenty-five of her passengers and crew were lost. In July 1886 the 1000 ton naval sloop *Amazon* collided with the Cork Steam Packet *Osprey*, which immediately sank with the loss of 10 lives.

The *Shambles* Lightship was stationed off Portland to warn of the dangers of the submerged shingle bank.

Avalanche & Forest: 11 September 1877

The 1154 ton iron sailing ship *Avalanche* was a fast clipper built in 1874 to take emigrants to New Zealand. On this occasion she was outward bound for Wellington with a thirty-four man crew and sixty-three passengers. A third of the passen-

The *Avalanche* was a fast clipper ship built in 1874 to take emigrants to New Zealand.

gers were returning to New Zealand following a visit to England. The *Forest* of Nova Scotia was a solidly-built wooden ship. Bound in ballast for New York, it was a third heavier than the sleek clipper.

Both vessels were tacking as they made their way down the Channel to the southeast of Portland within sight of the

Launching of the *Forest* in 1873 at E. Churchill & sons Shipyard, Hansport, Nova Scotia.

Shambles Lightship. A southwesterly gale was blowing creating heavy seas and poor visibility. The *Avalanche* was making about 7 knots when she caught sight of the *Forest* on the opposite tack doing about half that speed. Navigation lights on both ships were only glimpsed intermittently in the swell and it appears both masters expected the other to give way. When this didn't happen both captains, thinking they were taking avoiding action, actually turned towards each other setting their vessels on a fatal collision course.

At about 9 pm, with her bow high in the water, the *Forest* struck the *Avalanche* amidships like a battering ram and

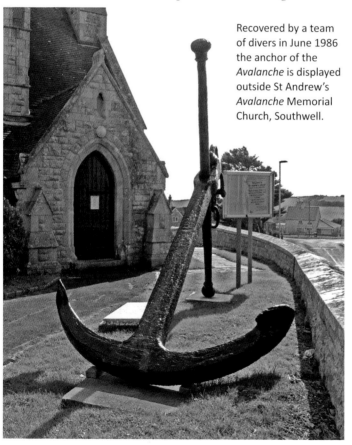

Recovered by a team of divers in June 1986 the anchor of the *Avalanche* is displayed outside St Andrew's *Avalanche* Memorial Church, Southwell.

A wealth of information about the tragedy is displayed inside the Memorial Church. The flag with the red cross of St George is the New Zealand 'Maori Flag', the one with the blue cross of St Andrew is an ensign from Nova Scotia where the Forest was built.

continued to rain blows along the side as the two ships passed. The force of the repeated collisions practically cut the iron ship in two causing her to keel over and the sea to pour in through open ports and hatchways. Within two minutes of the collision she was sinking. The carpenter and two other crew members on deck clambered on to the bows of the *Forest* but there was no hope for any of the people below decks.

Fearing she would also sink, all on board the *Forest* took to three boats but by morning only one boat survived with Captain Lockhart in charge. The Captain listened to advice from *Avalanche* survivor A.B. Mills. He was a local man, from Bridport who knew the dangers of Chesil Beach and advised standing offshore until daylight in the hope local fishermen would help them to land safely.

This was indeed the case. In appalling conditions Chiswell fishermen launched one of their 'lerrets', a boat especially designed and locally built to suit the unique conditions encountered on Chesil Beach. When the lerret reached the *Forest's* boat they found twelve exhausted survivors aboard. Realizing they would be unable to land with more than six extra men they signalled for assistance. A second lerret soon set off and having overcome the dangers of transferring the survivors between boats returned to the beach where a chain of rescuers was standing by. In this way all twelve men in the *Forest's* single surviving boat were brought to safety.

From the 22 crew members of the *Forest*, 11 died and there is scant memorial to them. Despite the bodies of five being identified at the time, all the men, including the carpenter of the *Avalanche*, were buried unnamed in a common grave. After lying in the loft of Chiswell 'Dead House' (see page 53), the bodies were placed naked in plain coffins for conveyance to St George's church-yard. It was left to the shocked Mrs Way of the Cove House Inn to lay her own white calico over the corpses.

The coffins were loaded on an ordinary four-wheeled cart without even any arrangement for pall bearers. Had passing quarrymen not downed tools to carry the coffins, they would have been tipped unceremoniously off the cart into the grave. *The Times* of London called the burial *'shocking and indecent'*. Rev'd Beazor squarely blamed the Coroner Richard Howard for not allowing proper resources and giving him sufficient notice.

The display cabinet inside the church entrance is full of artefacts brought up from the wreck of the *Avalanche* by a team of divers in the summer of 1984.

The loss of the *Avalanche* dealt a sad blow to many communities in New Zealand as a number of the passengers on board were returning home. Advice was later received in

This illustration of Portland fishermen in their lerrets landing the survivors of the *Avalanche* and *Forest* appeared on the front page of *The Illustrated London News*, 22 September 1877.

Wanganui from the vicar of St George's church, Portland that a piece of rising ground at Southwell had been purchased where it was proposed to erect a church to commemorate the gallantry of local fishermen and quarrymen. Subscriptions were invited from the people of Wanganui who helped partly fund the building of St Andrew's Avalanche Memorial Church. The church, purposefully erected with the front elevated towards the scene of the tragedy, contains a wealth of artefacts and is well worth a visit.

People took excursion trips from Weymouth to watch the navy's unsuccessful attempts to blow up the wooden hull of the *Forest*.

The derelict *Forest* remained afloat, partly submerged and a danger to shipping. The Navy was called in to destroy the wreck but several failed attempts using explosives left her even higher out of the water than before. Paddle steamers from Weymouth and Portland began running excursion trips out to the scene to witness the unsuccessful attempts to blow up the wooden hull. Eventually the Navy towed the wreck further down the Channel and blew it to pieces on 22 September.

The *Forest* grave and scant memorial in St George's churchyard Portland.

11

CHURCH OPE

Church Ope with its high cliffs and jagged rocks is about halfway up the eastern side of Portland. Like the rest of the island the coast here is particularly prone to fog, but partly sheltered from the ferocious southwesterly storms faced on the other side at Blacknor Point.

Paddle Steamer SS Bournemouth: 27 August 1886

Paddle steamers were once a familiar sight in British waters, both inland and around the coast. Predating railways by about three decades their introduction saw the beginning of mass tourism. One major attraction was the elegant saloon

The coast path at Church Ope follows the track bed of the disused railway line.

Church Ope with its high cliffs and jagged rocks is about halfway up the eastern side of Portland.

with licensed bar which, unlike pubs, was not restricted on opening hours. The railway created the Victorian seaside resorts by bringing visitors from cities and the paddle steamers entertained them when they arrived, providing pleasure trips as well as comfortable and affordable travel on coastal routes.

The sea-facing rocks have been left like jagged teeth after centuries of quarry working.

The paddle steamer SS *Bournemouth*, returning from an excursion trip to Torquay in 1886 struck the rocks at Church Ope in thick fog. It was travelling at full speed and had 194 people on board but only one lifeboat. The sea was relatively calm so there was no panic and no lives were lost. However, the steamer was abandoned and eventually wrecked.

The Paddle Steamer SS *Bournemouth* wrecked on the rocks at Church Ope on 27 August 1886. All the 160 passengers were rescued but the vessel became a total loss.

12

PORTLAND HARBOUR

The original harbour was naturally protected by the south coast of England, Chesil Beach and the Isle of Portland, providing refuge for ships against weather in all directions except east. The Royal Navy established a base at Portland in 1845, having gained parliamentary approval the year before to transform the harbour into a refuge. This was achieved by building massive breakwater arms or moles to encircle a surface area of 1300-acres. When completed in 1872 it was the largest man-made harbour in the world and is still the third largest.

The harbour, protected by the south coast, Chesil Beach and the Isle of Portland, provides refuge for ships against weather from all directions except east.

Portland Harbour continued to be a Royal Navy base until 1995. In choosing Portland, the Navy created a target at time of war. In his 1951 novel *The Cruel Sea*, Nicholas Monserrat – referring to warfare said *'man has made the sea crueller still'*. Portland bore testimony to this in both world wars.

Haytian: 18 February 1937

In 1910, following completion of another 2 mile section of the Portland mole the coal hulk *Haytian* was rammed and sunk in the harbour. After the wreck was raised in 1937 it was rammed again. The following press notice appeared in *The Gloucester Echo* on 18 February 1937:

'The patrol vessel H.M.S. P.C. 74 was badly damaged in the stern as the result of a collision with a coal hulk in Portland Harbour today. The coal hulk sank and only the top of a mast is visible. As far as can be ascertained there was no one on board the hulk. Tugs rushed to the scene, but the P.C. 74 took up her moorings without any apparent difficulty'.

The ill-fated coal hulk *Haytian* after it had been rammed in Portland Harbour in July 1910.

One of the salvage vessels that attended to provide assistance to HMS *PC74* was the steam tug *Portwey*. Built in 1927 for the coal bunkering trade along the South Coast supplying coal to steamers, she was also on-call for any ship requiring assistance. Today the *Portwey* is one of the National Heritage Vessels on display in London's dockland.

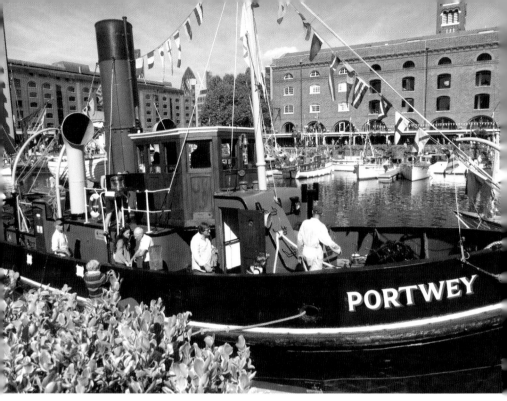

Today the steam tug *Portwey* is one of the National Heritage Vessels on display in London's dockland.

HMS *Hood:* 1914

From the time of her launch in 1891, the 14,150 ton armoured monster HMS *Hood* had become known throughout the fleet as a good looker but a terror to sail. She was weighed down with heavily armoured turrets which the First Sea Lord, Sir Arthur Hood, had insisted were installed to house her big guns. This extra weight lowered her freeboard so she needed dead calm to proceed at speed, otherwise great, green seas washed aboard covering the whole ship in clouds of spray, making gunnery impossible.

It is not surprising that shortly after her completion in 1893, the 380ft-long warship was sent to the calmer waters of the Mediterranean. She stayed there for nine years, was put on reserve duties and finally transferred to Portland as a target for torpedo practices. Her guns were taken out although they had never once fired a shot in anger.

On 4 November, 1914, shortly after the outbreak of WWI, HMS *Hood* was scuppered by the Royal Navy across the southern entrance to Portland Harbour, as a defence measure to prevent German U-boats firing torpedoes into the anchored Channel Fleet. She didn't go quietly. Once towed into position, the seacocks were opened in order for her to sink gracefully in an upright position. Unfortunately it took so long the tide turned and started to pull her out of place. Explosives were hurriedly used to blow a hole in the side but then she filled too quickly and did a port roll crashing completely upside down into the seabed. Her preserved condition, sheltered location and proximity to the surface meant she quickly became one of the UK's favourite dive training sites.

HMS *Hood* was the last of eight Royal Sovereign class battleships to be built.

HMS *Foylebank:* 4 July 1940

HMS *Foylebank* was a converted 5500 ton merchant ship active during the Second World War. Launched in 1930 she was requisitioned in September 1939 by the Royal Navy and converted into an anti-aircraft ship, equipped with 0.5 inch (12.7 mm) machine guns, two quad 2-pounder pom-poms and four twin high angle 4-inch gun turrets.

HMS *Foylebank* sinking in Portland Harbour on the 4 July 1940.

Jack Foreman Mantle, was posthumously awarded the Victoria Cross for his actions in defending HMS *Foylebank*.

The *Foylebank* arrived in Portland on 9 June 1940 for a build-up to anti-aircraft duties. On 4 July, whilst the majority of her crew were at breakfast, unidentified aircraft were reported to the south. These were originally thought to be Allied planes returning to base but turned out to be 26 Junkers Ju 87 Stuka dive bombers, one of the Luftwaffe's most feared attack weapons. The German squadron's intention was to disable the *Foylebank* which they identified as a threat to their plans to destroy Britain's coastal shipping.

In an eight-minute attack, two aircraft were shot down by the *Foylebank* but an estimated 22 bombs hit the ship. Shrouded in smoke she listed to port and sank the following day. 176 out of a total crew of 298 were killed. Many more were wounded. One of the ship's company, Jack Foreman Mantle, was posthumously awarded the Victoria Cross for his actions in defending the ship from aircraft attack whilst mortally injured.

13

WEYMOUTH & MELCOMBE REGIS

The town of Weymouth originated as a settlement on a constricted site south and west of Weymouth Harbour, an outlying part of Wyke Regis. By 1252 it was established as a seaport and became a chartered borough. Melcombe Regis developed separately on the peninsula north of the harbour and in 1310 was mentioned as a licensed wool port. Early in their history Weymouth and Melcombe Regis were rivals for trade and industry, but united in an Act of Parliament in 1571 forming a double borough known collectively today as Weymouth, despite Melcombe Regis being the main centre.

The wide stretch of Weymouth Bay on a calm summer day.

The resort emerged as one of the first modern tourist destinations, after King George III's brother, the Duke of Gloucester, built the grand residence of Gloucester Lodge in 1780 and enjoyed the mild winters here. The King made Weymouth his summer holiday residence on fourteen occasions between 1789 and 1805, even venturing into the sea in a bathing machine.

The magnificent East Indiaman *Earl of Abergavenny*, off Southsea in 1801 painted by Thomas Luny.

The Earl of Abergavenny: 5 February 1805

The *Earl of Abergavenny*, at 1180 tons was held in high regard as one of the largest East Indiamen in the company's eighty strong fleet. She was launched in 1796 and captained by William Wordsworth's brother John during her last two successful voyages to Bengal and China. There is some evidence that Captain Wordsworth was apprehensive about the 1805 voyage, possibly because he had £20,000 invested in 'private goods', including £1200 on behalf of his poet laureate brother William and their sister Dorothy.

The salary of officers in the East India Company was modest but made up for by the valuable perquisite of being allowed to ship 'personal cargo'. Many made fortunes out of their private trading. John's ambition for this voyage was to earn enough money to leave the sea, buy a property in Grasmere and help support William so he could devote his life to poetry.

The *Earl of Abergavenny* left East India docks during the early weeks of November 1804 to complete its loading at Gravesend and be in the Downs off Deal a few days before Christmas. The vessel's final port of call was Portsmouth, where most of the 60 passengers – men, women and children – boarded the vessel. With the crew and a number of East India troops there were 402 people aboard when it finally left the port accompanied by four other Indiamen, two whalers from Portsmouth and a naval escort provided by HMS *Weymouth* captained by John Draper.

The crew of the *Earl of Abergavenny* clinging to the masts and rigging as the vessel is overwhelmed.

On their passage through the Needles Channel the flotilla encountered strong, unfavourable winds and a signal was given by the convoy commander for all captains to take pilots on board and to make their way to Portland Roads. While waiting for a pilot vessel the *Earl of Abergavenny* struck the Shambles Bank where she was grounded for a few hours. At the turn of the tide, when she floated free it became clear her hull had been extensively damaged.

As the wind increased to gale force the first mate reported there was at least 12 feet of water in the hold.

William Wordsworth was deeply affected by the loss of his brother and went on to compose several poems in his memory; the last written in 1846, over forty years after John's tragic death.

Weymouth lifeboat *Friern Watch* drawing alongside the schooner *Ardente* after it had grounded in Weymouth Bay in December 1914. The five men on board were safely rescued.

Issuing spirits to the crew to encourage their efforts at the pumps seemed to have the opposite effect and they became 'most undisciplined'. Only at this stage was one of the ship's boats launched with the third mate, the purser and six seamen on board but they were never seen again.

There seems to have been a sad lack of urgency on the part of Captain Wordsworth who it appears believed the vessel could be safely beached on to Weymouth Sands. Not until 9 pm did he inform the passengers of the very serious situation. At about 11 pm the vessel gave 'a sudden lurch' and within minutes sank on an even keel in around 60 feet of water. This left some of the shrouds and about 25 feet of the main mast above the surface where passengers, crew and troops clung for dear life, but very few survived for long in the intense cold and piercing gale force winds.

WEYMOUTH & MELCOMBE REGIS

The *Earl of Abergavenny* sank just one and a half miles off Weymouth Esplanade. 261 of the crew and passengers died in the freezing water, while 141 survived by hanging to the mast and shrouds which projected above the surface for many months. Captain Wordsworth died with his ship. His body was eventually washed up near the town on 20 March and he was buried with nearly 100 others in a mass grave at Wyke Regis. For several months following the disaster strong rumours circulated that the Captain was to blame for not recognising the seriousness of the situation and taking appropriate action. William was deeply affected and went on to compose several poems in memory of John; the last written in 1846, over forty years after his brother's tragic death.

The 600 ton American ship *Robert* with its cargo of cotton on fire in Weymouth Bay in 1847 before drifting ashore near St Alban's Head.

By October 1807 several successful salvage attempts had recovered almost all the valuable property including 62 chests of silver dollars, 200 tons each of copper, tin, lead and iron in addition to cloth, haberdashery, millinery, glass, Wedgwood ware, harnesses, saddles and 30 pipes of wine etc. In September 1812 the wreck was blown up under water to prevent her forming a dangerous shoal.

L'Arguenon: 25 December 1930

An interesting sight for Weymouth residents out for a Christmas Day stroll in 1930 was the French Ketch *L'Arguenon* aground on the beach. The vessel was en route from Poole to St Malo and dropped her anchors on a windy night. Attempts by a naval steam pinnace to refloat her failed the following day but eventually, after lightening her ballast and with improvements in weather she was towed off.

The French Ketch *L'Arguenon* stranded close to the Weymouth Esplanade on Christmas Day 1930.

14

WYKE REGIS

Located on the northern shore of Portland Harbour at the southeastern end of Chesil Beach, Wyke Regis was originally a fishing village. Thanks to treacherous local currents and the long sweep of Chesil Beach on which many ships ran aground, Wyke gained a reputation for both smuggling and looting of wrecks. Today it has been swallowed by the urban sprawl of Weymouth's southwestern suburbs.

This 1693 chart shows the church at Weeke (Wyke) which enjoyed commanding views of Chesil Beach, the Small Mouth entrance passage to Fleet Water and the flourishing maritime town of Weymouth.

The fifteenth-century All Saints' church in the village was originally Weymouth's main place of worship and was frequented by King George III during his summer visits to the town between 1790 -1805. The churchyard has a melancholy maritime legacy with mass graves of victims from so many

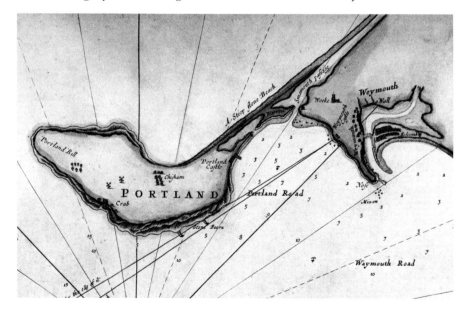

The fifteenth-century All Saints' church was frequented by King George III during his summer visits to Melcombe Regis between 1790 - 1805.

tragedies including the *Earl of Abergavenny* 1805 (see page 78) and six vessels from Admiral Christian's huge West-Indian-bound fleet of 1795 (see page 35).

The Golden Grape: December 1641

The *Golden Grape* Spanish treasure ship was driven ashore on the Chesil Beach across from Wyke in December 1641. The square topsail schooner, with a crew of twenty was bound from Spain to Dover with a fairy tale cargo. At Cadiz she took on board port and sherry wine, 2000 barrels of raisins of the sun, 400 jars of oil, two bags of red wool and forty three bolts of taffeta silk. From Cadiz she slipped surreptitiously into the bullion port of Sanlucar de Barremeda, the centre of trade for all the riches of gold and silver from South America. Here she loaded two bags of silver plate, a bag containing five hundred pistoles (Spanish two escudos gold coins later known as doubloons), and an unspecified number of bags of pieces of eight plus a peg and loaf of silver.

Leaving Spain she sailed back to Dover, but half way up the English Channel encountered a fierce storm and was swept up on to Chesil Beach where she sat for four days. Seven men and boys from her crew were drowned but the vessel did not break up. Despite the violent sea, country people from surrounding villages came with carts and packhorses to plunder the cargo, three quarters of which found its way into local cottages and farms. The authorities searched many homes trying to recover the goods and more than 400 locals were brought in for questioning.

> In memory of
> **JOHN WORDSWORTH**
> Commander of the East Indiaman
> 'THE EARL OF ABERGAVENNY'
> which on 5th February 1805, bound for Bengal
> and China, struck the Shambles Bank in
> Weymouth Bay and sank. Out of a total of
> about 400 passengers and crew, over 250
> perished, including John Wordsworth,
> younger brother of the poet,
> **WILLIAM WORDSWORTH.**
> John was buried in this churchyard on
> 21st March 1805. Other unnamed passengers
> and crew members, believed to be about 80 in
> number, are also buried here.
>
> This memorial marks the second centenary of the
> tragedy and was erected by the Wordsworth Trust,
> the Wordsworth Family and Friends

John Wordsworth, brother of poet William Wordsworth, lies in an unmarked grave together with around 80 passengers and crew of the East Indiaman *Earl of Abergavenny* sunk in Weymouth Bay on 5 February 1805.

As well as the surviving crew, over three hundred local inhabitants from the towns of Portland, Melcombe Regis and Weymouth plus the surrounding villages of Wyke, Chickerell, Fleet and Langton Herring as far as Abbotsbury, gave evidence about the shipwreck. In their sworn testimony they list what they had salvaged from the wreck and specified how they lived, giving details of their families, their homes and occupations. In doing so they mention another 200 like people.

Alexander: 27 March 1815

The East Indiaman merchant ship *Alexander* on passage from Bombay to London in 1815 was caught by a very strong gale from the south-southwest during the night of 26 March and was thrust upon the beach in front of Wyke village. None of the ship's officers survived and there were no witnesses to the disaster so the details remain unclear.

Early on the morning of the 27th, local inhabitants discovered a large quantity of wreckage scattered along the shore for several miles in both directions. Amongst this wreckage

The tombstone marking the mass grave of the officers who perished with Admiral Christian's Fleet in 1795 is now illegible.

was found the bodies of 39 East Indian lascar seamen and seven European officers and passengers. Five lascars were found alive; the only survivors from the 140 crew and passengers on board. Among the dead were Captain Lewis Auldjo, his wife Elizabeth and their daughter.

Local people collected the bodies on the beach for burial. The names of the dead lascars were lost with the ship's papers and they were buried in a mass grave in Wyke churchyard. The Europeans were identified soon afterwards and buried under a memorial erected near the church tower.

This wall memorial by the church tower is in memory of the souls lost on the *Alexander*, the East Indiaman wrecked opposite Wyke on 26 March 1815.

LULWORTH COVE

Lulworth Cove is a natural harbour whose existence is owed to the same collision of continents which created the Alps. This beautiful secluded inlet provided a welcome refuge for vessels caught in a channel storm.

Among those ships unable to make it to safety are two separate records eleven years apart, of unidentified vessels both being swept onto farm land. The first one in 1734 mentions '*a small wrecke having been thrown upon*' a farm at West Lulworth. The second episode, recorded in 1745, details an unidentified wreck washed up on 23 October on land belonging to Hamburrow (Hambury) Farm, West Lulworth. The debris included the masts, sails, blocks and '*small cordage of small value*'.

Lulworth Cove is a beautiful secluded natural harbour.

A 'Moody' 36' yacht similar to the ill-fated *Caroline of Leigh* which sank 3 miles off Lulworth in December 1979 with the loss of four lives.

Dove: 24 December 1697

On two separate occasions, one in 1734 and another eleven years later, there are reports of vessels being washed up on West Lulworth farms.

The *Dove* carrying a cargo of wine was wrecked off Lulworth on Christmas Eve during the severe winter of 1697-98 when coastal ice built up to 8 inches in parts.

Unknown Sloop: 12 February 1758

On 12 February 1758 an unknown sloop bound from Weymouth to Portsmouth with a cargo of malt was lost off Lulworth. All on board were drowned.

Vigilante: 14 December 1825

From the diaries of shoemaker Henry Rolls of East Lulworth, we learn the *Vigilante* was wrecked a little west of Lulworth Cove on 14 December 1825. Rolls, born in 1803, kept a journal of the main happenings in the village throughout his adult life. After his death in 1877, his wife, and later, his daughter, continued to keep the journal up to date.

The *Vigilante* was laden with barley for Africa which suggests it could have been involved in the slave trade. There were seven men and a boy on board but only one man was saved by being hauled up the cliff with a rope. Eight years later, when Henry Rolls was thirty, The Slavery Abolition Act came into force and slavery was abolished throughout the British Empire.

Caroline of Leigh: 18 December 1979

A 'Moody' 36' yacht *Caroline of Leigh* sank 3 miles off Lulworth while heading for Bordeaux on 18 December 1979 with the loss of four lives.

To Lulworth fishermen the threat to life by shipwreck was ever present.

Looking across Worbarrow Bay to the cliffs and ridge of Flower's Barrow.

16

WORBARROW BAY

Worbarrow is a very broad and shallow bay just east of Lulworth Cove. At the eastern end is a rocky promontory known as Worbarrow Tout and towering over the north is Flower's Barrow ridge which, due to coastal erosion, is gradually falling into the sea. Worbarrow is only accessible to coast path explorers when the army ranges at Lulworth are open to the public. The bay can be accessed down an easy track from the car park alongside the ghost village of Tyneham, whose residents were forced to leave their homes in 1943 when the area was requisitioned by the War Office. The residents of Worbarrow suffered a similar fate and today little evidence remains of the eight cottages and coastguard station that once stood close to the bay but the buildings can be glimpsed in the painting *Shipwreck in Worbarrow Bay* by prominent marine painter Clarkson Stanfield (1793-1867).

GWR Steamer South of Ireland: Christmas Day 1883

On Christmas Day 1883 the *South of Ireland* (GWR) Great Western Railway steamer was wrecked on the rocks at Worbarrow Bay. In 1871 an Act of Parliament had permitted GWR to operate ships in connection with their trains. The services operated between Weymouth, the Channel Islands and France on former routes served by Weymouth and Channel Islands Steam Packet Company. Smaller GWR vessels were used as tenders at Plymouth and the River Severn and River Dart ferry routes.

At the eastern end of the bay is the rocky promontory known as Worbarrow Tout.

In *Shipwreck in Worbarrow Bay* by Clarkson Stanfield, the former fishermen's cottages and coastguard station can be glimpsed below the headland of Worbarrow Tout.

Black Hawk Liberty Ship: 29 December 1944

Liberty ships were a class of cargo vessel of simple, low cost construction, mass-produced in the United States during World War II. Built on an unprecedented scale the 7100 ton freighters came to symbolize US wartime industrial output and formed the backbone of the Atlantic convoys.

Liberty ship *Black Hawk* was torpedoed by German U-boat U772 on 29 December 1944 when 7 miles southeast of Portland Bill Lighthouse. Captain William Leroy Bunch was in command of the last ship in the starboard column of a two column convoy when attacked by the U-boat. Two liberty ships, *Arthur Sewall* and *Black Hawk* were torpedoed and both damaged beyond repair. Shortly after the attack the U-boat itself was sunk by the escort.

Thirty minutes after the attack, *Black Hawk's* complement of seven officers, 34 men, 27 gunnery guards and an Army Security Officer began to abandon ship in four boats and two rafts. They were picked up by HMS *Dahlia* and landed at

Brixham in Devon at 20.30 hours. Four men were injured and the cook died ashore in hospital.

Later a salvage crew boarded the vessel to prepare her for towing to Worbarrow Bay, where she was beached the following day and declared a total loss. Today the remains of *Black Hawk* provide a very popular dive site, due to its proximity and relatively shallow depth, making it suitable for divers of all grades.

Black Hawk liberty ship was torpedoed seven miles southeast of Portland Bill Lighthouse, the stern section was towed and sunk in Worbarrow Bay.

The 150 million year old black clay cliffs of Kimmeridge Bay.

17

KIMMERIDGE BAY & LEDGES

The roughly semi-circular bay with its low 150 million year old black clay cliffs lies a mile southwest of Kimmeridge Village and is accessed via a toll road. The natural limestone ledges extending out into the bay make it a wonderful location for rock pooling but also a sinister hazard to shipping. The Fine Foundation Marine Centre here explores the exceptional sea life found on this part of the coast, and features interactive displays and a variety of aquaria.

Wreck of the Welfare: 1371

One of the most notorious of all Dorset shipwrecks occurred in 1371 when a large crowd of locals plundered the wreck of the *Welfare*. Sailing from Dartmouth en route to London the vessel ran into difficulties off Portland and was driven aground on the rocky ledges at Kimmeridge.

The ship's cargo included 32 pieces of gold cloth and richly embroidered silks together with other valuable merchandise. Edward III called a commission and tried no fewer than a hundred people for their part in robbing the ship. At the trial in Sherborne, Master of the *Welfare*, Robert Knolles, testified he had been molested by robbers who had been cajoled by Abbot Thomas of Cerne Benedictine Abbey into storing the cargo in a building at Kimmeridge.

As owner of the Manor of Kimmeridge the Abbot had 'Right of Wreck' to the shore. However, although the vessel had

Treacherous limestone ledges at Kimmeridge are wonderful for rock pooling, but a sinister hazard to shipping.

This ship is similar to the *Welfare*, wrecked in 1371 and plundered by locals.

run aground she was still held by her crew, which meant pillaging of the ship was unlawful. Six years later, in 1377, the Abbot was himself was eventually convicted along with the other accused.

Stralsund: 8 December 1872

In 1872 the five-oared lifeboat *Mary Heape* was based at Chapman's Pool under the captaincy of William Stickland. During a gale on 8 December she was called out to rescue the crew of the *Stralsund*, a German ship blown onto Kimmeridge Ledges during a terrific gale. After two attempts the *Mary Heape* succeeded in rescuing the whole crew, seventeen in number.

Cerne Benedictine Abbey owned the Manor of Kimmeridge and '*Right of Wreck*' to the shore. Today this Gatehouse is all that remains of the Abbey.

18

CHAPMAN'S POOL

Chapman's Pool is a small cove cut into the steep cliffs near the imposing bluff of St Alban's Head. As with Lulworth Cove the sea has eroded the hard outer rocks and is now rapidly (in geological terms) scouring away the softer limestone to form a horseshoe shape. Chapman's Pool however lacks the near-complete enclosure of Lulworth but does have a rugged untouched quality. Unlike Lulworth there are no shops or visitor centre, in fact nothing much more than a huddle of fisherman's huts and a few small boats.

Georgina, French Barque: **11 July 1866**

On the 11 July 1866 the French barque *Georgina* of 400 tons was driven ashore at Chapman's Pool. Her crew of thirteen

The horseshoe-shaped bay of Chapman's Pool with Houns Tout Cliff towering in the background.

This French barque at anchor is similar to the *Georgina* wrecked at Chapman's Pool in July 1866.

and two passengers were saved by a rocket line fired to the ship by coastguards. When the weather calmed her cargo of coffee, cocoa and mahogany was largely unloaded but the ship was destroyed.

This was not the only instance of shipwreck and the decision was taken to build a lifeboat station here. A newspaper of the time commented: *'the great loss of life and property on this part of the coast have at length aroused the attention of the government and we are happy to say that there are preparations for placing a lifeboat station in this little bay.'*

The boathouse was built very close to the actual place where the *Georgiana* was destroyed but the lifeboat station was short-lived. It closed in 1880 because of the expense of maintaining the boathouse, and the fact it was too far from any settlement to be manned quickly. It was also difficult to launch from here in a strong wind. In 1868 when the schooner *Liberty* got into difficulties off Broad Bench (the western end of Kimmeridge Bay), it proved impossible to launch the lifeboat into the teeth of the gale and the boat was wrecked. Although the station closed over a century ago, the boathouse can still be seen, in its lonely position at the foot of Emmetts Hill.

SS *Treveal:* 9 January 1920

The loss of cargo steamer SS *Treveal*, and 36 of its crew of 43 was possibly the worst shipwreck off the Purbeck coast in the first half of the twentieth century. Owned by the Hain

Steamship Company of St Ives, the vessel's crew consisted mainly of Cornishmen. At the time the doomed freighter went aground approaching St Alban's Head, she was making for Dundee on the return leg of her maiden voyage to Calcutta with a cargo of jute and manganese. The delayed response of the crew in sending out distress calls and firing flares, combined with the severe weather conditions, diminished any hope of salvation. A dockyard tug did put to sea from Portland, only to get into difficulties itself and be beaten back by the gale. Through the night and the following dawn coastguards at St Alban's Head and Kimmeridge were aware of the vessel's presence but not the danger she was in. The same was true of the Worth Matravers volunteer life-saving company.

A model of the *Thomas Markby* with sails hoisted can be seen bottom left of this display cabinet in Swanage lifeboat station.

Additional tugs and lifeboats were on hand at Portland, Weymouth and Swanage and the following morning another two were sent, one towing the Weymouth lifeboat but by this time the storm had intensified. Just when it seemed the

A sister ship to the SS *Treveal*, owned by the Hain Steamship Company of St Ives. All Hain's steamers displayed the H symbol on the smoke stack.

The *Treveal* broke completely in two and both halves sat on Kimmeridge Ledge throughout the spring and summer of 1920.

lifeboat might be overwhelmed, it was swept away to safety, eventually finding shelter in Poole Harbour. Meanwhile the *Treveal's* master, Captain Charles Paynter of St Ives, seeing the ship had split along its side, gave the order to abandon ship. The crew got away in two boats and rowed for the shore but 50 yards from the beach capsized and only seven of the 43 crew reached the shore alive. Captain Paynter was among the men who lost their lives in the churning surf.

The seven survivors were pulled from the waves by Rev'd M. Piercy, the Vicar of Worth Matravers, with the assistance of local villager Frank Lander. The young clergyman had taken over the parish in 1916 from the lately deceased Rev'd James Edwards but as the First World War progressed he left to become a stretcher bearer in the Royal Army Medical Corps, declining the commission he could have had as a Cambridge man. When the war ended he returned to Worth and without his intervention and that of Frank Lander, the seven survivors would almost certainly have been dragged to their deaths by undertow on that fateful morning.

The survivors were put up at the Anchor Inn in Swanage while the mangled bodies of their captain and crewmates were collected from the beach and taken in farm carts up to the village where they were laid out in the Reading Room (now Worth Matravers Tea & Supper Room).

Two young servicemen Will Corben and Herbert Hooper, natives of Worth Matravers, were given the grim task of digging a mass grave and interring the corpses. Before they had laid the last body in the trench news was received that the bodies were required to be sent to Cornwall for burial in St Ives. Fifty years later Will Corbin could still recall the events of the weekend in detail:

'That day we fetched up over a dozen, in a wagon from Renscombe Farm. They was three deep in the wagon. With us and all it was a fair load. Took a team of good horses to get it up to the village'.

'I was on top of the heap, unloading, when a lady come by an give me a telling off for trampling on the dead. I said "They'm past minding, missis, and so am I". She didn't like that a bit. Come into the graveyard later on and ticked off Herbie for swearing in the presence of God. Well, by that time we'd had enough. We'd shifted a mountain of earth and banked it up against the wall while the bodies were laid in the trench. Just before the order came to take 'em out again the whole bloody lot fell in.'

'We'd had enough. Herbie looked down at all you could see of a good ship's company under mud and stones, most in the prime of their lives, and he said, "If God's listening, I don't reckon he's got much to be proud of". 'She didn't get much change out of Herbie and me'.

Unidentified body parts and two bodies of unknown sailors from the *Treveal* crew lie buried beneath this mound of earth in the north east corner of Worth Matravers churchyard.

In January 1920 this building served as a temporary macabre mortuary. It is now The Worth Matravers Tea & Supper Room,

An inquest was held in the village pub, The Square & Compass and later, a week long enquiry took place at Stanley Hall in Weymouth. However, the secret of how the SS *Treveal* became so far off course and stranded on Kimmeridge Ledge is lost forever in Chapman's Pool.

Turkie: 20 October 1939

On 29 October 1939 the Greek Steamer *Turkie* was wrecked at Houns Tout Cliff near Chapman's Pool. The crew were saved by the Swanage lifeboat *Thomas Markby*, which remained on duty for 74 hours. The *Thomas Markby* was on service at Swanage from 1928 until 1949 and during that time they attended 67 call outs and saved 27 lives. A model of the lifeboat can be seen in Swanage lifeboat station.

An inquest into the *Treveal* tragedy was held in The Square & Compass pub in Worth Matravers.

19

St Alban's Head

The promontory of St Alban's Head (a corruption of St Aldhelm's Head) is located 3 miles southwest of Swanage and is the most southerly part of the Purbeck peninsula. Looking west from here there are dramatic views along the coastline with a series of scarred white cliffs rising vertically from thick undercliff vegetation. Crowning the headland the thirteenth-century St Alban's Chapel was built on the site of a much earlier Christian hermitage, but the current building is a nineteenth-century restoration. St Aldhelm, a noted Latin poet and ecclesiastical writer, was Abbot of Malmesbury and Bishop of Sherborne at the end of the seventh century.

From St Alban's Head there are dramatic views along the coastline looking west, with a series of scarred white cliffs rising vertically from the thick undercliff vegetation.

St Alban's Chapel on the promontory seems more likely to have been a secular watchtower for Corfe Castle, covering sea approaches to the south, rather than a place for worship.

The building has several unusual architectural features for a chapel; the square shape, the orientation of the corners towards the cardinal compass points, and the division and restriction of the interior space by a large central column. This, together with the lack of evidence for an altar or piscina suggests it may not have been built as a chapel at all but as a watchtower for Corfe Castle, covering the sea approaches to the south.

Royal West India Mail Steamer Tyne: 24 January 1857

The Royal West India Mail Paddle Steamer *Tyne* ran aground at St Alban's Head on 24 January 1857. Fortunately for the crew, the ship wedged itself between two of the limestone ledges. All were saved having been advised by coastguards to stay aboard until daylight.

Montanes: November 1906

All on board the *Montanes* were rescued when she became stranded in fog at St Alban's Head in November 1906. The steamer was carrying silver ores, manganese, canary seed, cork, wine and oranges – hundreds of which bobbed on the surface of the sea the morning after she was wrecked.

The Royal West India Mail Paddle Steamer *Tyne* on shore at St Alban's Head 24 January 1857.

L'Atlantique: 5 January 1933

Built in St Nazaire, for service between France and South America, this floating palace of a ship was launched on 15 April 1930. She could carry 1238 passengers; 488 first class, 88 second class and 662 third class. She was designed with a largely art deco interior on an unusual axial floor plan including a hallway up to 20 feet in width on each passenger deck

The *Montanes* became stranded in fog at St Alban's Head in November 1906. All on board were rescued.

105

and a foyer at the centre of the ship three decks high. Interior decorations were largely of glass, marble, and a variety of woods, making for a subdued atmosphere.

On 5 January 1933, while she was sailing between Bordeaux and Le Havre to be refitted, there were just crew members on board. The vessel caught fire in the Channel and her demise was watched from the Purbeck cliffs. One onlooker on St Alban's Head had a sextant and recorded her position as 50° 34′ N -20° 3′ W.

Luxury liner SS *L'Atlantique* engulfed by fire off St Alban's Head in 1933.

The blaze, believed to have started in a first class stateroom, was discovered by the ship's crew around 3:30 in the morning. The fire spread rapidly, and by first light captain, Rene Schoofs, ordered the crew of 200 to abandon ship. Four freighters responded to a distress call, the SS *Achilles*, a Dutch steamship, rescued almost the entire ship's complement. During the afternoon, *L'Atlantique* began listing to port and on 5 January the French Ministry of Merchant Marine issued a statement saying she was considered a total loss.

The *Sunderland Echo and Shipping Gazette* (6 Jan 1933), reported that on 4 January 1933 Thomas Henry Willmott, of Sunderland, first mate of the SS *Ford Castle* collier, was in charge of the lifeboat which went alongside the burning liner at considerable risk to pick up the few survivors who had been overlooked by other rescuing ships. For this courageous act he was awarded the 'Medaille de Sauvetage' by the French Ministry and presented with a gold watch by the ship's owners.

The liner was towed to Cherbourg, where the fire was extinguished on 8 January. She remained docked while the ship's owners and insurers debated her demise, eventually resulting in the payment of US$ 6.8 million to Compagnie de Navigation Sud Atlantique for the loss. In February 1936, she was sold for scrap, and broken up by the firm of Smith & Houston in Port Glasgow.

The first class art deco dining room of the SS *L'Atlantique*.

Aeolian Sky: 3 November 1979

Early morning on 3 November 1979 the 14,000 ton Greek freighter *Aeolian Sky* was steaming southwest of the Isle of Wight, bound for Dar-es-Salaam. The sea condition was rough and a steady force 6 to 7 wind was blowing from the southwest. At the same time the much smaller 2400 ton German MV *Anna Knueppel* was heading up Channel in an easterly direction. At 4.55 am the vessels collided and, rather surprisingly, the smaller ship escaped virtually unscathed. However, the *Aeolian Sky* was holed near the bows and started to take on water into the forward hold. She was just a year old with her hull and machinery valued at over £3 million, not including the cargo in her holds, or the many containers and dozens of Land Rovers on her deck.

The 'Medaille de Sauvetage' was awarded to Thomas Henry Willmott, of Sunderland, for his bravery in rescuing crew members from the SS *L'Atlantique*.

The Master requested the urgent assistance of a tug and the *Abeille Languedoc* put to sea from Cherbourg but before she arrived the situation turned critical. The second bulkhead had given way, and number one and two holds were full of water with the remainder of the ship open to the sea leaving no option but to abandon ship. A call went out to the Royal Naval Air Station at Lee-on-Solent for a helicopter. Sixteen crew members were air lifted to a Dutch naval destroyer standing by to render assistance.

When the tug arrived at about 8 am, a salvage inspector went aboard while the evacuation of the crew continued; transferring the remaining men to the tug by means of an inflatable boat. A line was secured to the stern of the stricken ship and the tug took her in tow towards Southampton.

The bows were almost under water and deck cargo was breaking free and floating away. Drums containing poisonous chemicals including paint and thinners, liquid chlorine, butane aerosols, Bostic cleaner and ammonia were soon being washed ashore along the coast of the Isle of Wight and a major danger alert was put into operation. In addition to the toxic cargo and Land Rovers the ship was carrying glass and barbed wire.

Due to the very real possibility of the ship sinking while under tow and cause major shipping problems in the Solent, the decision was made to switch the destination to Weymouth Roads but early next day, amid gale force winds and huge seas, the *Aeolian Sky* sank 5 miles from St Alban's Head in just over 100 feet of water.

On 18 January 1980, ten weeks after the loss of the *Aeolian Sky*, a firm of London loss adjusters contacted Dorset Police and revealed part of the ship's cargo had been a consignment of 60,000,000 brand new Seychelles rupees with a sterling value £4,500,000, stored in the sickbay for want of anywhere else to put them. A team of specialist divers were engaged and despite reaching the correct location in the vessel there was no trace of the twelve numbered wooden cases containing the notes.

The police began tentative enquiries among the fishing and diving fraternity, which led to a fisherman from the Lulworth area being visited. He handed over four 100 Seychelles rupee banknotes which he acquired a few days after Christmas 1979. He stated he found them inside his lobster pots that had been strung out on the sea bed 5 or 6 miles south of Lulworth Cove.

The *Aeolian Sky* after she had collided with the *Anna Knueppel*. The lettering on her stern is her name in Greek.

Dorset Police then liaised with Interpol to circulate details of the missing notes to appropriate continental banks and also for crew members of the *Abeille Languedoc* to be interviewed. Crown Agents arranged for the military to search beaches in the vicinity of Lulworth Ranges to see if any notes had found their way ashore but none were found. Detective Superintendent Antoine of the Seychelles Police travelled to the UK and accompanied Dorset Police detectives during the course of many enquiries.

60,000,000 Seychelles rupees (Sterling value £4,500,000) are still missing from the wreck of the *Aeolian Sky*.

Following media coverage and issuing of a press release, a small number of people, living as far apart as Portland and the Isle of Wight, came forward to volunteer they were in possession of one or two of the missing notes. Each told similar stories as to how they came by the notes: they had all been recovered from the sea at various places between Lulworth and Hengistbury Head. Some had been brought up in lobster pots, some trawled up in fishing nets. These notes had all been recovered during January and February 1980. Examination of the serial numbers confirmed they came from a total of nine of the original twelve packing cases. In 1996 police learnt two of the notes had been included in the estate of a deceased Somerset farmer and were to be sold at auction in Tavistock, Devon.

20

Winspit & Seacombe

The site of the *Halsewell* wreck. With the help of local quarrymen 82 survivors somehow managed to climb the vertical cliffs to safety.

The magnificent, showy ships of the East India Company were the aristocrats of the maritime world making long hazardous voyages to bring home exotic goods from the other side of the globe. Over a period of 29 years three of these prestigious vessels were lost on Dorset's coast. The *Alexander* and *Earl of Abergavenny* are well known, but the wrecking of the outward-bound *Halsewell*, seems almost more shocking and has acquired a legendary significance.

A newspaper illustration of survivors from the *Halsewell* attempting to climb the precipitous Seacombe Cliffs.

On New Year's Day 1786 the 785 ton vessel set sail from Gravesend for Madras. The commander Captain Richard Pierce was the company's most senior officer. Planning to retire after this final voyage he had invested heavily in personal trade goods to take full advantage of the company's prerequisites for its officers.

The total ship's complement was around 240, made up mainly of crew and a number of newly recruited troops going to serve in various East India garrisons. There was a relatively small number of passengers on board including one gentleman and seven beautiful young ladies deliberately despatched to India in the hope of attracting husbands. Two of the innocent girls were the captain's own daughters Eliza and Mary Ann, a further two were his nieces, Amy and Mary Paul of Somerset.

The voyage began badly. As the *Halsewell* approached Dover Straits on Monday 2 January snow and ice fouled the topsails and rendered the mainsail virtually useless. On Tuesday, as the ship lay at anchor, a strong east northeast gale threatened to drive her into the Kentish cliffs. Cables were cut and she made for open sea. During the evening the wind intensified shifting to the south and by now the gun-deck was awash. By eight o'clock on Wednesday morning the situation had worsened. A westerly gale increased the amount of water forced the hawse-holes in the bows and a leak in the hull was discovered: *'all the pumps were set to work'*.

In the cuddy of the doomed ship Chief Officer Henry Meriton looks on as Captain Pierce tries to comfort his daughters and the other young ladies.

The mizzenmast was cut down and further attempts made *'to wear the ship'* but the coxswain, and four others drowned during this desperate bid to turn the vessel from the wind. Two feet of water was pumped from the hold but it was realised continuing to India would be impossible. The crew bent another foresail, raised a *'jury main-mast, and set a top-gallant-sail for a main-sail'*, in an effort to limp into Portsmouth for repairs.

Progress was painfully slow. Twelve hours later the ship successfully passed Portland Bill, intending to round the next trio of treacherous headlands of Anvil Point, Durlston Head

and Peveril Point hoping to anchor in the relative shelter of Studland Bay. Instead, at eleven o'clock that night, the sky cleared and the great promontory of St Alban's Head loomed a mile and half to the leeward. Sails were immediately drawn in and the sheet anchor dropped. Asked by Captain Pierce to give his opinion of the situation, Chief Officer Henry Meriton shook his head saying there was little hope of saving lives: '*as they were then driving fast on the shore, and might expect every moment to strike*'.

A mirror from the *Halsewell* hangs above the door in the church at Worth Matravers.

A ship's cannon fired distress signals to alert those onshore to the predicament. The anchors were lowered but dragged and in the early hours of Friday morning the *Halsewell* struck the rocks at the foot of Seacombe Cliffs, at a point about halfway between Winspit and Dancing Ledge: '*with such violence a shriek of horror burst at one instant from every quarter of the ship*'.

A seaman named Burmaster climbed through a skylight in the roundhouse and waved a lantern. From this faint light Henry Meriton noticed a spar from the side of the ship resting on the rocks. He attempted to escape but was carried off by a surging wave which then washed him up onto a shelf at the back of a cavern in the cliffs.

Included in the small museum at The Square & Compass pub in Worth Matravers is this display case presenting the story of the *Halsewell* and including some artefacts from the wreck.

The remaining officers took refuge on the upper quarter-gallery on the poop deck where they heard '*the ladies shriek at intervals, as if the water had reached them, the noise of the sea at other times drowning their voices*'. In the cuddy, Captain Pierce hugged his daughters, praying the stricken ship would hold together until dawn, when rescue might come and escape routes could be seen. The hull, however, was splitting apart.

Meanwhile, 27 men found refuge on what is now known

as the Halsewell Rock and struggled from there to join Meriton in the cavern above. Several *'perished in their efforts'* but those who found refuge had escaped immediate death although now had to endure the cold and perpetual dousing with icy spray. During the night the cook and quartermaster managed to scale the perilous cliff and reach Easington Farm, waking the steward of the local quarry owner. The quarry-men were marshalled by Mr Garland, a stone merchant from Eastington, who sent for vital ropes and tackle.

Hope was now at hand but the worse was by no means over. In order for the men to reach the extended ropes they had to crawl along an exposed ledge *'scarcely as broad as a man's hand'* then turn a corner and climb vertically. The cliffs are worse than vertical here, with a 'declivity' of 8 feet inwards to the crucial point from which the survivors were

Over a period of 29 years three of the magnificent, showy ships of the East India Company were lost on Dorset's coast.

hauled to safety. This was overcome by two quarrymen risking their lives to lean out from the outcrop and lower a second rope with a noose, which the would-be survivor put around his waist, then was drawn up the jagged rock-face. The quarrymen carried on pulling up seamen and soldiers for the whole day and returned at dawn on Saturday 7 January, for the last man – William Trenton, a soldier – who had managed to withstand extreme hypothermia. In all, 88 men were recovered but fourteen died in the process.

All the ship's documentation was lost and cargo and debris floated across a wide area. The total death toll was 166 including Captain Pierce and his daughters and nieces. Henry Meriton wrote an account of the disaster as did John Rogers, the other chief-officer. Many years later Charles Dickens embellished the story for an article in *Household Words*, entitled 'The Long Voyage'.

The coast path is clearly marked.

The jagged Purbeck coastline passes Anvil Point lighthouse and turns north at Durlston Head.

EAST PURBECK

Anvil Point is located at the eastern end of limestone beds stretching from St Alban's Head in the west to Durlston Head in the east. Anvil Point Lighthouse, situated within the grounds of Durlston Country Park, is approximately 2 miles up hill from Swanage town centre. The light is positioned to give a waypoint for vessels on passage along the English Channel coast. To the west it gives a clear line from Portland Bill and to the east guides vessels away from the Christchurch Ledge leading them into the Solent.

From Anvil Point the coast bears north to face the waters of Poole Bay. Along its jagged route to the Foreland at Handfast Point are the rocky hazards of Durlston Head, Peveril Point and Ballard Point. With a little imagination the profile resembles a sharks head with Swanage Bay the gaping mouth.

Wild Wave of Exeter, a brigantine like this, was wrecked on Peveril Ledge in a southerly gale on 23 January 1875.

Wild Wave: 23 January 1875

The brigantine *Wild Wave* of Exeter was wrecked on Peveril Ledge in a southerly gale on 23 January 1875. At 5 a.m when distress rockets were fired she was on her beam ends. After tremendous efforts, made during the night before a wintry dawn, four men and a boy were rescued by Coastguards in four-oared open boats. Poole's lifeboat *Daylight* was towed round Peveril Point by the steamer tug *Royal Albert* but after struggling through gales for 7 miles, arrived just as the survivors were taken off.

Charles Robinson, of Newton Manor House, Swanage, who witnessed the incident from the shore, wrote to The Times: *'Swanage has hitherto had no lifeboat, but after this morning's work we shall supply that want.'* He described how Coastguards took out two boats, but could not get near enough and how, at daylight, '...*five dark sodden bundles, rather than living creatures were seen, all clustered together, clinging to a mass of tangled rigging, at the highest part of the ship's hull.'*

He detailed how, when wind moderated and shifted a point or two, the Coastguard boats were manned again.

'Soon we see a coil of rope thrown from the largest boat and caught by one of the living "bundles" on the ship's hull, and in a few minutes (thanks be to Heaven!) all five – one a very small one, a poor little benumbed lad of 10 or 11 (who had been washed off once and caught again by the 'scruff' of the neck like a drowning dog) were safely stowed in the boat.'

Adding a postscript to his letter Robinson said: '*Now, Sir, I have written this account less to record the excellent discipline, efficiency, and gallantry of the Swanage Coastguard, than to call attention to the urgent needs of the district and the adjacent coast. It will scarcely be believed that along all the line of the coast of Dorset and Hants, from Portland to Hurst Castle, there is not a single lighthouse nor a single harbour of refuge!'*

The present day *George Thomas Lacy* lifeboat. The wall boards in the background detail over a century of service in local waters.

Charles Robinson, together with George Burt of Purbeck House, Swanage both gave £20 towards a fund for establishing a lifeboat. The National Lifeboat Institution acted on the suggestion and lifeboat *Charlotte Mary* was on station at Swanage by September. Over the following fifteen years she attended 11 services and saved 18 lives. A model of *Charlotte Mary* is displayed in the present lifeboat station.

Looking across Swanage Bay from the lifeboat launching slip towards Ballard Dow with Old Harry Rocks in the background.

Alexandrovna: 29 April 1882

On 29 April 1882, with her topsail in ribbons, a hurricane drove the 1250 ton Liverpool sailing ship *Alexandrovna* towards the cliffs below Swanage lighthouse. No crew was seen and the ship eventually struck Ragged Rocks west of Round Down. Such was the storm's force in the ten minutes it took would be rescuers to reach the spot, the ship had been reduced to driftwood. The entire crew of 77 perished, many bodies being later found wedged among rocks or drifting in the Channel. One naked corpse recovered from the sea was still attached to a lifebuoy and it was only this and discovering the ship's empty boat, that enabled the vessel to be identified.

HM steam drifter *Plantin:* 26 April 1917

The 84 ton wooden steam vessel *Plantin*, was hired by the Admiralty in 1915 as an armed net drifter. On 26 April 1917, she was engaged in minesweeping just off Old Harry Rocks in a minefield laid by the German U-boat UC-72 under the command of Oberleutnant Ernst Voight. The *Plantin* fouled a mine which detonated beneath her destroying the ship, The *Plantin* sank immediately with the loss of nine men including the forty-seven year-old skipper John Wood and his two sons John, twenty and William eighteen. Only one man survived and no bodies were recovered.

The Aparima: 19 November 1917

At the outbreak of WWI the Admiralty requisitioned a cargo liner from New Zealand as a troopship. The 5704 ton SS *Aparima* was defensively armed and crewed by officers, cadets and lascars from the Union Steam Ship Company, New Zealand; although in November 1917 she was flying the British flag and was under the command of Captain Gerald Stokely Doorly.

The SS *Aparima* seen here departing Wellington in 1915.

When in service as a troopship the *Aparima* was renowned for being a slow traveller managing a maximum speed of only 12 to 13 knots.

On 19 November 1917 she was sailing from London to Barry in South Wales to take on a load of coal. As she made her laborious way down the English Channel, Captain Doorly took her in as close to the coast as he dared and set a zigzag course. Both measures were designed to give the ship the best opportunity of avoiding U-boat attack but proved in vain. Passing the Isle of Wight, holding a course about 4 kilometres southwest of Anvil Point, German U-boat 40 under the command of Oberleutnant Hans Howaldt fired a torpedo in to her port side. The sudden explosion occurred at about 12.50 a.m. and within eight minutes the *Aparima* was sunk. 56 of the 110 crew were tragically lost. Among them were men from Britain, India, Australia and New Zealand plus seventeen cadets whose sleeping quarters had been close to where the torpedo struck.

Officers of the ill-fated steamer *Aparima*, including some who were lost when the vessel was torpedoed in the English Channel in November 1917.

The Kyarra: 26 May 1918

Built at Dumbarton by William Denny and Brothers for the Australian United Steam Navigation Company, The *Kyarra* was a 6953 ton cargo and passenger luxury liner. She was launched on 2 February 1903 on the River Clyde and for ten years sailed between Fremantle and Sydney. Her name was taken from the aboriginal word for a small fillet of possum fur.

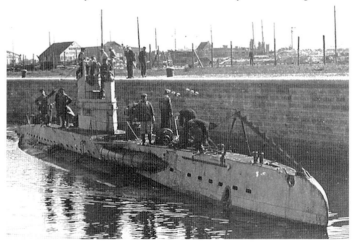

On 6 November 1914 she was requisitioned and converted into a hospital ship for the purpose of transporting Australian medical units to Egypt. The hull was painted white with a large red cross on the side.

The SS *Kyarra* was one of many allied vessels to fall victim to torpedo attack in British waters.

In March 1915, she was converted into a troop transport and on 5 May 1918 sailed from Tilbury to Devonport, to

A U-III class submarine of the type that sunk the SS *Kyarra*.

Torpedo special-
ist Oberleutnant
Johannes Lohs
who sank some
150,000 tons of
Allied shipping
during his mili-
tary career.

Born in Trinidad,
Captain James
Gerald Stokely
Doorly, survived
the sinking of the
Aparima by
jumping over-
board and being
picked up by one
of the lifeboats.

embark civilian passengers and take on full general cargo. However, when rounding Anvil Point on the morning of 26 May 1918 at 8.50 a.m. disaster occurred. In a calm sea Captain Albert Donovan spotted the wake of an approaching torpedo and immediately tried taking avoiding action but it was too late. The order to abandon ship was given and lifeboats were winched down as the *Kyarra* began to sink. In twenty minutes she had disappeared beneath the waves.

As well as 2500 tons of cargo including wine, cloth and perfume there were more than 140 people on board. The torpedo strike killed five crew members immediately, injuring another so badly he died later. The SS *Kyarra* was one of many vessels to fall victim to torpedo specialist Oberleutnant Johannes Lohs, captain of German submarine UB-57 who sank some 150,000 tons of Allied shipping during his military career.

For years the *Kyarra* lay 30 metres below the sea providing a home for a myriad of marine life, until scuba diving became increasingly popular in the 1960s. The wreck was bought for sport diving in 1966 and is now one of Dorset's most dived wrecks.

STUDLAND BAY

Studland Bay sweeps round from Old Harry Rocks at Handfast Point to the entrance of Poole Harbour. Three chalk formations, including a stack and a stump, mark the most easterly point of the Jurassic Coast, World Heritage Site. They are named after local pirate, Harry Paye.

Continuing north past the rocks is a glorious expanse of natural coastline featuring a 4-mile stretch of golden sandy beach, with gently shelving bathing waters and views of the Isle of Wight. Towards the end of January 1866 a storm in the usually peaceful waters of Studland Bay wrecked three

Studland Bay is a glorious expanse of natural coastline featuring a 4-mile stretch of golden sandy beach.

schooners. Eighteen people were drowned and there were only two survivors.

The Studland Bay Wreck

In 1984, following a chance discovery by a fisherman, marine archaeologists recovered some timbers from a Spanish Galleon which had been rotting in Studland Bay at Handfast Point off Old Harry Rocks for nearly 300 years. It is one of only a handful of shipwrecks from the era of Columbus to have been found.

Originally thought to be the wreck of the *San Salvador*, one of the Spanish Armada ships, this is now considered unlikely. Instead it is thought to be a merchant vessel from Spain, possibly trading in the first quarter of the sixteenth century. A possible candidate is the *Santa Maria de Luce*. A number of ballast stones identified as coming from the Basque region of Spain, plus recovery of a Basque pottery jug point to the

Three chalk formations at Handfast Point are known as Old Harry Rocks and mark the most easterly point of the Jurassic Coast, World Heritage Site.

ship's area of origin. This was a vessel from the era of exploration when Europeans were discovering parts of the so-called New World for the first time.

Some of the most important objects found on the Studland Bay Wreck are now on display in Poole Museum including one of the few firmly dated wrought iron guns salvaged in British waters. Other objects include a water pump made of walnut wood, used to clear water from the ship's bilge. This life-saving piece of equipment is a very rare find. Large amounts of early sixteenth-century pottery have been recovered alongside more personal artefacts and possessions like wooden bowls, a medicine bottle with stopper still in it and a nit comb – an essential piece of kit for any seafarer at that time.

This model of the Studland Bay vessel made by Ron Burt was commissioned by Poole Maritime Trust and is on display in Poole Museum.

Constitution: 17 January 1879

On 17 January 1879 '*the boom of guns quickly made known the fact that the American old three-masted vessel, the Constitution, had in the haze and mist of the night*' found herself aground on shingle near Old Harry Rocks. The United States frigate was carrying products from France for the Paris Exhibition on the other side of the Atlantic.

When morning came, guns, chains, cable and other heavy articles were removed to lighten her and around five steamers spent several hours trying to pull her clear. Eventually a Government tug arrived from Southampton, and together with the steamers, they were able to release the *Constitution*, and tow her to Portsmouth where only minor damage was found.

A wealth of artefacts from the Studland Bay Wreck in Poole Museum include animal bones, pottery pots, pans, and jugs, wooden platters and bowls, a leather shoe and a nit comb.

Annie Margaretta: 24 January 1879

Exactly a week after the *Constitution* foundered near Old Harry Rocks the 500 ton Norwegian timber schooner *Annie Margaretta* ran into the headland within a few hundred yards of the same spot. The Scandinavian vessel had also left France for America. By afternoon however she was a total wreck later selling for £45 at auction.

Because of the force of a heavy sea driven in by easterly wind the Swanage lifeboat *Charlotte Mary* had found difficulty getting down the Peveril slipway to aid the *Annie Margaretta*. The Lifeboat Institution later decided to build a groyne to hold back the sea.

An artists' impression from the *Illustrated London News* of the *Constitution* aground off Old Harry Rocks in 1879.

The car ferry (bottom right) crosses the entrance to Poole Harbour linking Studland and Sandbanks.

SANDBANKS – SWASH CHANNEL

The Swash Channel is the name given to the deep water strait that provides maritime access between Poole Bay and Poole Harbour. West of the channel lies the ancient anchorage of Studland Bay where ships waited for the right weather conditions to either enter the harbour or sail out into the English Channel.

On the eastern side of the Swash Channel is the Swash Bank, part of the notorious Hook Sands which have for centuries been responsible for innumerable wrecks. The loca-

The highly regarded Sandbanks Beach where property and land values are fourth highest in the world.

tion of the sands can be discerned from Studland Beach by a line of frothing white disturbance on the sea's surface.

The Swash Channel Wreck

The Swash Channel Wreck was discovered in 2004 during survey work for deepening of the main shipping channel into Poole. The wreck site contained an almost complete side of the ship with associated material spread over an area of 40 by 50 metres, including very rare decorative wooden carvings indicating the high status of the vessel. This led to the largest under water excavation since that of the *Mary Rose* in the 1980s.

The ship was found to be heavily armed for a merchant vessel with at least 26 carriage-mounted guns, suggesting it could also have served as a warship. Analysis of the ship's timber showed it was cut down in the Netherlands or

Germany in about 1628 and the type of pottery found was produced in the Netherlands between about 1625 and 1650. Further research suggested the ship is most likely to be the

The location of the notorious Hook Sands can be discerned from Studland Beach by a line of frothing white disturbance on the sea's surface.

Research into the Swash Channel vessel suggests it is most likely to be the *Fame* from the port of Hoorn north of Amsterdam which sank whilst at anchor in Poole Bay in 1631.

The magnificent carved head of a man on top of the ship's 8.5 metre high rudder is on display at Poole Museum.

Fame from the port of Hoorn north of Amsterdam. In 1631 she was on a voyage to the West Indies sailing under Captain Jacob Johnson Botemaker with a crew of 45 when she was caught in a storm off Hook Sands and capsized whilst at anchor.

The upper parts of the ship were decorated with wooden carvings, a number of which have been recovered. They are the earliest found on a wreck in British waters and among the earliest in the world. One of them is the magnificent head of a man on top of the ship's 8.5 metre high rudder. His countenance is reminiscent of figures depicted in paintings of the Dutch Golden Age. A wide range of domestic objects, tools, navigational equipment and ships fittings were also recovered many of which are now on display in Poole Museum.

The carved rudder or 'whipstaff', hinged from the ship's stern post, was the method used in sixteenth and seventeenth-century Europe to control the movement of a large sailing ship.

BIBLIOGRAPHY

Maureen Attwooll: *Discover Dorset Shipwrecks*

Edwina Boult: *Christian's Fleet – A Dorset Shipping Tragedy*

Philip Browne: *The Unfortunate Captain Pierce & the Wreck of the Halsewell, East Indiaman, 1786*

David Burnett: *Dorset Shipwrecks*

Nigel Clarke: *Shipwreck Guide to Lyme Bay for Divers & Skippers*

Poole Museum Heritage Series: *The Studland Bay Wreck*

David Pushman: *The Loss of the SS* Treveal

Steve Shovlar: *Dorset Shipwrecks*

Graham Smith: *Hampshire & Dorset Shipwrecks*

Selwyn Williams: *Treasure of the Golden Grape*

Terry Townsend's other Halsgrove titles include:

Once Upon a Pint – A Readers' Guide to the Literary Pubs & Inns of Dorset & Somerset

Bristol & Clifton Slave Trade Trails

Jane Austen's Hampshire

Jane Austen & Bath

Jane Austen's Kent

Kent Smugglers' Pubs

Dorset Smugglers' Pubs

Hampshire Smugglers' Pubs

Isle of Wight Smugglers' Pubs

West Cornwall Smugglers' Pubs: St Ives to Falmouth

East Cornwall Smugglers' Pubs: Kingsand to Mevagissey

Suffolk Smugglers' Pubs

East Sussex Smugglers' Pubs

More Dorset Smugglers' Pubs

East Devon Smugglers' Pubs

Wiltshire's Haunted Pubs & Inns